The American Affair
with Openness

THE AMERICAN AFFAIR
WITH OPENNESS

▼

What the Left Unleashed from Pandora's Box

Scholar Spartacus

iUniversity Press
San Jose New York Lincoln Shanghai

iUniversity Press
an imprint of iUniverse.com, Inc.

For information address:
iUniverse.com, Inc.
5220 S 16th, Ste. 200
Lincoln, NE 68512
www.iuniverse.com

ISBN: 0-595-17458-2

Printed in the United States of America

What is a man? what has he got?/
If not himself, then he has not/
To say the things he truly feels/And not the words of one who kneels;
The record shows/ I took the blows
And…did it…**my way.**

—Frank Sinatra

CONTENTS

▼

FORETHOUGHT

▼

I see problems that are seemingly inherent within a politically correct open society. I sense that many others see the rising problems as well but for many reasons are too shamed and hesitant to pursue solutions. Yes, fearful and hesitant—not confused and divided, as we shall see. The ideology of political correctness pervades all realms of our daily lives. The fervent uneasiness it affects needs to be addressed. Therefore, without a degree to my name or several decades of experiences to my life, I, a little undergraduate, came to sit down and respond with a series of reasons explaining why I was at odds with this thing called Openness. In the spirit of W.E.B. Du Bois "I pray you, then, receive my little book in all charity, studying my words with me, forgiving mistake and foible for sake of the faith and passion that is in me, and seeking the grain of truth hidden there." While this project was not produced as romantically as, say a manifesto during imprisonment, the following essays (polemics) did initially spring from persistent dissatisfaction and sincere unhappiness with college and certain current events.

This whole venture really began because I was feeling academically unmotivated and unfulfilled. I hated going to most of my classes because I found most of them boring. To me, the quantity of class participation ('discussion') was high but its quality low, i.e., trite, ambiguous (cautious), disengaging. Rarely was there an oasis between comments either too shallow to bother pondering or so 'deep' that symbolism was to be found even in the article, "an."

I felt like I was being slowed down but not for the reasons you have probably arrived. It is not that I am so smart and prodigious over my classmates or fancy myself such. Rather it seemed to me the readings were not taken as seriously by most others as they were by the fingerful of us. On the other hand, I chauvinistically love my college and most everything about it. I desire a bachelor's degree from no other institution. Hence my conflict. What's a frustrated student to do? Leave school? (No, not practical.) Seek therapy? (No, not necessary.) Editorialize—rant—in the campus paper? (Maybe but not worth the time investment.) Begrudgingly tolerate it? (No, not helpful.) Drink? (Yes, but not for solace. A more constructive outlet can be found.) A journal? (Hmmmmm....)

This initially began as a pet project, something of a catharsis, if you will, to stimulate my scholarship and writing skills, which as I have said, I felt were not being humored by my curriculum. I intended on pitching the scribblings. But a funny thing started to happen: the thoughts kept pouring out, my pens were running out of ink, and I was running out of space in the notebook—and I was liking it. Still, it was not until the pages grew more numerous that I realized my original intent of just scribbling out my thoughts had blossomed into several distinct yet interrelated interpretations on the shortcomings of political correctness in an open society. Could it be that I was actually on to something? I remember thinking to myself, I might have a critical perspective, here. Exxxcellent.

This *critical perspective* (note the *italics*!) is immensely enthused with classical liberalism and inspired by works done by Ayn Rand, Daphne Patai, Robert Bly, and Allan Bloom to name a few. In my little book of essays I focus on the purported values of Openness with its relativism, cultural relativism, and political correctness. In each essay I try to offer a contrary perspective on how a vigorous and diverse civil and free society ought to be sans Openness.

Introduction:
On Openness

Since it is unavoidable to the greatest part of men, if not all, to have several opinions, without certain and indubitable proofs of their truths; it would, methinks, become all to maintain peace and the common offices of humanity and friendship in the diversity of opinions. We should do well to commiserate our mutual ignorance, and endeavor to remove it in all the gentle and fair ways of information; and not instantly treat others ill, as obstinate and perverse, because they will not renounce their own, and receive our opinions.

—John Locke

Openness is not what it appears to be, or maybe it is and therein lies the problem. The virtues of the Openness philosophy are its very same shortcomings, principally trying to please everyone all the time and never wanting to offend anyone any of the time. The internal contradictions make impossible any practical realization of its aim, especially without compromising constitutional and tacit rights. Its unattainability, however, is not the issue at hand. If that were the case then it would be unworthy of the effort given to address it as a great many constructs in our lives can never really be fully contained and stored in some jar or warehouse. Therefore its unattainability makes it ordinary, common, without novelty.

Also because so many more concepts—some of greater import, even—
have unattainable ends, if not more so, I would be wrong and deficient for
singling out Openness from its host of competitors. No, the issue at hand
is Openness' illusory and confounding objective, campaign, ideals, and
inventions to which we are coerced in giving way and, in some respects,
yield to. By we I mean in particular American society and, on the whole,
the world, lest the reader forgets we are living in what Michael McLuhan
coined a global village. I am not so much disputing the fancies of
Openness as I am its application of the law (force) because, like supporters
of various other social schools of thought, it has a right (for lack of a better
word) and place round the debate table to advertise and peddle its various
ideas. I can not often make sense of the whole thing but in the supposition
of Socratism I acknowledge that what is not intelligible to me is not
necessarily unintelligible.[1] Still, I dispute its social combinations imposing
on society norms by forcing us to accept them directly or indirectly "if we
find them contrary to our best interest or repugnant to our consciences."[2]
Frederic Bastiat said that one has the cruel alternative of losing one's moral
sense or losing one's respect for the law when law and morality contradict
each other.

Society is imposed on directly and indirectly by the infinite wails of
discomfort and hurt feelings. America is being made to feel guilty for
everything under the sun. In an ironic play of events she is receiving
counseling therapy by the same camp intellectual elite responsible for the
finger pointing, or, as they like to phrase it: *"making us aware..." "making
us open to..."*

Firstly, what is openness? Definitively, according to the **American
Heritage Dictionary** (1994) openness means, among other things: *afford-
ing unobstructed entrance and exit; not shut or closed...having no protective
cover...having gaps...unrestricted...susceptible; vulnerable...frank; candid...to release from a closed or fastened position...undo...to get (something)
going; to make more responsive or understanding...come into view.* The
reader will forgive the parade of definitions, for it is necessary to show the

connection between the definitive word and the philosophy. The philosophy of Openness is exactly the practiced embodiment of all things listed above. This is not, in and of itself, bad. At one point in time Openness was designed to make us clear-eyed to other cultures and ourselves. Its means to this end was through teaching reason, reflection, and knowledge in place of myth and passion.[3] The pedagogy required serious thought and analysis of natural rights so that one would be capable of defending his opinion (and rejecting another's).

The new Openness with us today, enthused with cultural relativism, is, however, "progressive and forward-looking," making light of history and democratic principles, leading us to a state of detachment and indifference under the guise of indiscriminate tolerance and diversity. It is specious. The whole movement rejects reason and fairness. It is overly concerned with emotions, feelings and being politically correct. I realize it is of little use to argue for the return of the old Openness, for the effects of change are irreversible. Therefore, understanding Openness' virtues *in theory*, the following sections will attack and criticize its actual effects in practice.

The following series of essays explore and critique the unintended and intrusive negative consequences of, perhaps, well-intended efforts to establish political correctness on an open society in America.

"Too Open for Our Own Good" critiques how the current Openness threatens standards and expectations by its advocation of a free-for-all/anything-goes-forum. To this fire of relativism (or is that, absolutism?), all other things are like oxygen, fodder to its insatiable, indiscriminate consumption. Since it 'affords unobstructed entrance and exit; not shut or closed' every belief, every person, every thing is equally equal. Custom A and Custom Z are both correct. Nothing is never below something. (This claim of tolerance and acceptance, like so much of Openness, is illusory). Since Openness is friend to everything it has 'no protective cover'—possibly thinking, "Cover from what? Why would anyone harm his *friend*?" Yet, one cannot truly be a loyal friend to this person and sponsoring his pro-choice endeavors let's say while simultaneously supporting another's pro-life endeavors. Is it honorable or ethical for a manager to bet on his boxer and his boxer's opponent? If the involved parties have any sense they will wonder exactly on whose side this character is seriously aligned. From this perspective, Openness turns out to be more of a foe than a friend because it takes neither party seriously and treats each with indifference.

Trying to please, or more accurately, not offend, anyone any time is one of the prevailing features of current Openness. I find it unappealing and cowardly. It is unbecoming of leadership. The world is simply filled with too many '–isms' to have them all accepted, too many people to expect them all to get along, too many biases to be fully understood, flavors to be appreciated, opinions to be tolerated. In the truest sense of the word one must discriminate if only to learn differences. It is a part of reasoning and survival to juxtapose and evaluate. Openness on the other hand seeks only to homogenize, to show similarities however miniscule and romanticized they may be. Ironically, and I know no other way of putting it save to say, That's Openness, it dogmatically advocates diversity, encouraging fractionalization among students, politics, and labor. There is a party for poor people, for mothers, for homosexuals; there are parties for war veterans and another for homeless veterans, for old people and for young people, for immigrants, and each ethnicity defends its legitimacy to a separate party. What is more, each fraction works to show how and why its differences make it special. That is fine. The problem, as I see it, enters when you overestimate your special-ness without taking into account that other people may think likewise of themselves. This problem is further fanned when diversity is practically mandated in effect creating a pseudo fraternity. By and large, any union bonded involuntarily, i.e., legislated and forced, is a structure waiting to implode. A house divided against itself cannot stand. Which are we celebrating: our similarities or our differences? Unless you are a progressive liberal you realize the two cannot be done at the same time any more than a man can at the same time be free and not free.

To overly celebrate the similarities would lend more to union but eventually contest individuality and liberty. To overly celebrate the differences would lend more to diversity but would create a climate where each group attempts to outperform the others with its particular philosophies and cultural or racial uniqueness. College campuses all across the nation can attest to the latter. Mr. Bastiat wrote: "Mr. De Lamartine once wrote to me thusly: 'Your doctrine is only the half of my program. You have stopped at liberty; I go on to fraternity.' I answered him: 'The second half of your program will destroy the first.'"[4]

The fence that Openness straddles on most issues makes it 'vulnerable' to its clear-eyed critics. Citing the resolution of the "so-called student 'rebellion' " (original quotations) at the University of California at Berkely in 1965, Ayn Rand affirmed in *The New Left* that compromises do anything but satisfy everybody. "It does not lead to general fulfillment, but to general frustration," reiterating my earlier belief that "those who try to be all things to all men, end up by not being anything to anyone."[5] She goes on to remark that a little victory for an unjust claim only serves to encourage the claimant further.

The principal scope of Openness is to not offend anyone in the effort to please everyone all of the time. Sounds good, n'est pas? Perhaps too good to be true? That which is too good to be true usually turns out to be so plus trouble. The toll for accepting every philosophy, lifestyle, ideology, cultural custom (save patriarchal, oppressive American traditions) is absolute mitigation or indifference. It is not so much that the person is as openminded as he boasts in as much as he is indifferent to most. Openness is a grand whitewashing machine. Consequently one thing is never better than another is. They may be different but they are essentially the same. Different but equal. Odd. Where have we heard that before?

"United Fishbowls of America" deals with this new Openness' threat to privacy. My contention is that not all circles of our lives need be or should be open to public knowledge and scrutiny. It is simply not merely a matter of a private life but the many subsections of privacy like romance, fun and games, familial issues, personal health, friends, sex, emotions, age (in some cases), income, unpopular or silly habits, personal problems, opinions, convictions, ideas, preferences.

Clearly, some occupations—show business, politics, professional sports, for example—conditionally sacrifice or forfeit some fancies of privacy for the sake of prominence or fame. Other occupations like espionage, Navy Seals, scientists, (and some politics still) must need utmost secrecy or anonymity. Perhaps some of those subsections of privacy seemed anachronistic to you. Well, this comes as no surprise to me. After all, fewer and fewer boundaries are acknowledged, and entertainment pervades literally every venue of America. What this translates into is an almost automatic dismissal as antiquated anything with a hint of strictness. In addition, the mere presence on television or accompaniment of audio/visual effects are enough to transfigure any matter into being just a show. The distinct line that once separated the private from the public has virtually been erased into oblivion. True to the tune of socialism Openness does not allow division.

"The Intangibles" highlights the threat Openness poses to conviction and honesty. Supposedly the elite of scholarship, some professors leave the impression that devoutly held convictions are the essence of un-enlightenment or narrow-mindedness, and "that uncertainty and skepticism are socially valuable traits which would lead to tolerance of differences, flexibility, social 'adjustment' and willingness to compromise," securing a "peaceful, 'democratic' society."[6]

What has happened to straightforward answers and opinions from students and private citizens? Clearly, spinning is no longer just a campaign or advertising tool. One would think that with the growing diverse diversity of "talk" shows and shock jocks, electronic voyeurism, gay pride parades, and the ubiquity of surveillance cameras, regular folks would be unrestricted—open—with their views? After all it seems there is very little to hide and even fewer remaining sanctums. Alas! such is not the case. People are becoming more afraid to say what they genuinely mean;

fear of being called racist, sexist, chauvinist, close minded, old fashioned, insensitive keeps sincerity at bay. People are wary of being sincere for fear of losing favor and being branded politically incorrect. One has only to ask a question requiring a thoughtful, never mind rational, response to perceive the pervading influence of Openness. I believe the reader would be hard pressed to get any reply outside of "Who am I to say what is right or what is wrong?" "I can't pass judgement;" "That is for God to decide" (as if to imply they actually worship God or that God exists). Or the reply may fall along the line of "I would not do it but if they want to then that's fine." Worse still, "It's different but…"

To quote Allan Bloom, "Thus what is advertised as a great opening is a great closing."[7]

The philosophy promotes 'frank or candid' discussion. The frankness it encourages is many times too raw for the ears of most and amounts to what I consider articulated gutter-talk lectured from a pair of specs with a college degree. (From my observation the prevailing attitude is, indeed, frank but more closed, i.e., one sided than open. Left liberals often dominate the "dialogue" as they tend to be more loquacious and passionate about their opinions which they all to often mistake as maxims. By no degree do I imply liberalism hogs the microphone. My liberal-minded classmates and others simply are more apt to speak up. Perhaps those with opposing views are not so much pressured and fearful as they are dispassionate and unsure of their ethos, in which case it is better they keep quiet than exhibit their ignorance and foolishness through empty rationale though through silence it is implied the opposition are condonable.)

Keeping in line with the definitions listed, proponents are on a mission to 'undo' and 'release from a closed or fastened position' every secret, established system, and individual belief or as they might rename them: fear, big bully America, bigotry. Any civilization or society that is experiencing marked unraveling of the basic family values and structure, its religiosity, language and customs is experiencing tremendous change with an uncertain future. For example, the American stalwart of hard work and persistence is debatably ebbing into antiquity. Hey, what can't be had when it is wanted is worth suing over to get.

The essay "Why XY?" examines Openness' threat to masculinity. This threat to maleness is exhibited through "heterophobia"[i], anti-biology propaganda, the disappearance of male initiations and bastions, gay-rights activism, and the ever-expanding grounds for sexual harassment. For instance, by the mere say-so of a woman, any male gesture can be offensive and cause a lawsuit. In further threatening masculinity and heterosexuality, Openness, specifically through feminism, seeks to undo our general conception of biology by introducing the "third gender" to mainstream America. We are witnessing a prevalent urge for alternative lifestyles to exit the closet 'from their closed position' and be vividly open.

"Open Warfare" explains why Openness threatens patriotism. Openness defenders are typically suspicious of tradition, secular in faith, liberal in everything. They can find nothing right in the American way of life. They trounce conservatism and discretion. Is this tolerance? "We are making you more aware," they say. "We are not here to change you, just make you understand," they coo. All of which society holds to be private or immoral and taboo or even patriotic for that matter is attacked and scrutinized before being inevitably denounced. Questioning, my good reader, is not bad; it is a mark of cognition and true scholarship. Immanuel Kant, in "What is Enlightenment?" argues that questioning must never be discouraged. Be an absolute tyrant all you want, says he, but never under any circumstance dissuade your people from questioning. But questioning for the sake of questioning and then being intolerant of any answers offered is annoying and characteristic of intelligence gone sour. What begets complaining for the sake of complaining?

---

i Daphne Patai uses the term "heterophobia" to describe the meaning of antagonism toward "the Other—in the present context men in general—and toward heterosexuality in particular"(*Heterophobia*, 5).

Despite the commendable aim 'to get (something) going; to make more responsive or understanding' modern education is quick to shut out ethics, biology, and community standards. Anything that presents a counter view is obviously closed minded and, therefore, stupid and prejudiced. Typically, what is esteemed patriotic, i.e., traditional, is dragged through the mud of rhetoric and shamed into being evidence of America's evil capitalist patriarchy. In truth, if with its strong current of relativism Openness could elect a position and cease equivocating, then the listener might recognize that he will not only 'learn' something but also be expected to agree with it. From the perspective of Openness, listening and understanding are synonymous with agreeing; if you don't agree, then you obviously were not listening. (Or, in the spirit of Openness the listener could probably get away with not agreeing with them, which is not the same as disagreeing with them.) As far as the recent education of Openness is concerned, the only enemy is the man who is not open to everything.[8]

In summation, the following writings were penned to highlight the eroding effects of political correctness on open society in the United States. My hope is that other undergraduates may find some solace or encouragement for staying true to themselves and their morals amidst the peer pressure of indifference and cynicism.

[1] Frederich Nietzsche, author of *The Birth of Tragedy*, trans. Walter Kaufman (New York: Vintage Books, 1967), section 14, 93.

[2] Frederic Bastiat, "The Socialists Reject Free Choice," *The Law*, trans. Dean Russell, (New York: The Foundation for Economic Education, 1998), 64.

[3] Allan Bloom, author of *The Closing of the American Mind*, (New York: Simon and Schuster, 1987).

[4] *The Law*, 21-22.

[5] Ayn Rand, author of *The New Left: The Anti-Industrial Revolution*, (New York: Signet Non-Fiction, 1970), 37.

[6] Ibid., 27.

[7] *Closing*, 34.

[8] *Closing*, 27.

Too Open for Our Own Good

―――――▼―――――

Until all teachers are geniuses and enthusiasts, nobody will learn anything, except what they teach themselves.

—"Antic Hay" by Aldous Huxley

The most important thing about goals is having one.

—Geoffry E. Abert

Threat to Standards

Americans love winners and outstanding individuals. We love heavily decorated heroes (and not so heavily decorated heroes, too), back-to-back victors and reigning title defenders. We also admire and cheer on the underdog. Doubtless there is some empirical research that sheds light on this phenomenon but let it be sufficient to say Americans like upsets; seeing the little guy take on the big man *mano y mano*…and win (see *Mr. Smith Goes to Washington*, 1939). It is true, we like latter day David and Goliath endings, e.g., labor unions fighting big business; a new official replacing the incumbent; U.S. Women's Soccer team winning the championship (especially in a sport more widely enjoyed outside of the

States) or Jamaicans forming an Olympic bobsledding team. Stories like these inspire us. Maybe they even remind us of the *potential* each of us has to unleash in the name of accomplishment. America stands as the sole world superpower. Ain't it grand? As boxing promoter (and personality extraordinare) Don King always says, "ONLY IN AMERICA!"

For there to be a champion means there has to be a loser. To appreciate and admire the underdog means there has to be a seated top dog. In Plato's *Statesman* the Stranger speaks to Young Socrates thus: "Do you not agree that in the nature of things 'the greater' can be so called only in relation to the less and to nothing else; and, conversely, that 'the less' can only be 'less' than a greater? It cannot be less than anything else." He goes on to amend this statement with further qualifiers but for the purpose at hand the only standard applicable is that of relative comparison, thus ruling out the possibility of a 'greater' minus a 'lesser'.

In short, there must be a contrast; something with which there can be some glaring juxtaposition. Thus stands (or looms) a standard to be met and surpassed. Is it not reasonable the reigning champion is the standard? Agreeing upon this, it follows that it is up to the contender to meet that standard and surpass it. This idea is easily illustrated through the contest King of the Hill. In wrestling practice we almost always play this game wherein the objective is to stay out on the mat as long as possible, taking down each challenger until you, yourself, have finally been taken down. I realize the world is not a huge athletic event. Nor is the world one huge stage and yet we understand Mr. Shakespeare's point. I used examples of sport and competition to introduce the visible risk Openness poses to distinctions and standards.

Openness is a threat to conventional standards. Standards are written or understood sets of expectations. Some of them were established some time long past, and in addition to being measures of distinction they are also products of tradition to which I am convinced Openness is clearly opposed. Openness is a threat to standards by: (1) placing everyone in the same boat of capabilities and talents; (2) opting to lower rather than raise expectations; (3) catering to the lowest common denominator; and (4) exercising more tolerance than chastisement.

The first way in which this philosophy threatens standards is by its insistence on placing everyone in the same boat. Refusing to discriminate (in the true sense of the word) skill levels, capabilities, characteristics, and interests, means that individuality is not acknowledged. Fortunately, people have various propensities, dispositions, talents, and, in some cases, innate gifts and genius which, if cultivated properly, will eventually distinguish the individual from the common. Every human being is not another face in the crowd. There are those among us who are truly one in a million. These few, for the exceptional or outstanding is never in the majority, do not deserve to be stripped of their special-ness and lumped in with Joe Anybody. To do so would constitute an injustice to individuality, ambition, the "I"! Ayn Rand's *Anthem* superbly illustrates the extreme consequences of collectivism with the deletion of the word (and concept of) "I." Throughout the novella, the protagonist refers to himself as "We"; there are no identities, no names; no Ryans, no Cindys, no Zacharys, no Lindas, no Davids, no one.

This movement towards sameness, which bemusingly is done under efforts toward diversity, is dissimilar to the axioms within the *Declaration of Independence*: *"We hold these truths to be self-evident that all men are created equal."* Are Mr. Jefferson's words being improperly construed by PC ideologies? Yes. That all men are created equally is self-evident of a wonderfully optimistic (Enlightenment) and Christian doctrine that God loves and forgives all his children in equal abundance; each soul is blessed with life by the Almighty. "Gary Wills, in his study of the Declaration (*Inventing America*, 1978), tells us that Jefferson means *equal* in possessing a moral sense: 'The moral sense is not only man's *highest* faculty, but the one that is *equal* to all men.'"[9] The sentiment also appeals to Nature. In the recent past the biological union of man and woman reproduced all people (in a separate essay—"Why XY?—I critique the advancing science of eugenics and modern fertilization technology). Supernatural forces conceived none but Jesus Christ.[ii]

Thus, the American Declaration asserts that we all are **created** equal, not that we all are equal. Perhaps this subtle but significant difference is what kept Mr. Jefferson from abolishing slavery?

Efforts to equalize our talents are a difficult task and one in which success would surely come via mandate. The very attempt, let alone legislation, is an attack on liberty. It is an injustice to paralyze the faculties of some so that others will benefit. Such efforts are done in the name of parity, association, diversity, and democracy. Placing everyone in the same class of capabilities and talents makes two miscalculations. The first miscalculation is that we all are equal in our endeavors, potential, and make up. Generalization of this sort threatens individuation. Each must make the most of the one life given to us and that encompasses effectively using our God given endowments and reaping come what may from hard work and training. For life to run its appointed course we must apply our talents, i.e., gifts and faculties, to our surrounding natural resources and convert them into products for use. Success, said Zig Ziglar, is the maximum utilization of the ability that you have. Mr. Bastiat said, "We hold from God the gift which includes all others. This gift is life— physical, intellectual, and moral life...Life, faculties, production—in other words, individuality, liberty, property—this is man. And in spite of the cunning of artful political leaders, these three gifts from God precede all human legislation, and are superior to it."[10]

Whenever the system, regardless of the motivations, takes from the haves (be it intellectually, physically, monetarily)—minus compensation

---

[ii] The myth of an earthborn people during the reign of Kronos tells that the rotation of life went backwards towards youth. Every day and night the race of people grew younger and younger until they simply withered away, returning as Christian burial rites pronounce ashes to ashes; dust to dust. Born of the cosmos they return to it. This may be read in Plato's *Statesman*, Chapter Three.

or consent—and gives to the have-nots so now the have-nots have, then the presiding powers have committed what many libertarians appropriately term legal plunder.

The second miscalculation in the pattern of creating equality is setting the standard by the underprivileged—the have-nots and contenders. Is it not more beneficial to standardize as high as possible? Hypothetically speaking, is it more worthwhile or, at least more desirable, that we all be wealthy or that we all be poor? In wanting to literally put everyone on the same level, having them perceive themselves identical, what practical effect is actually produced by schools that no longer recognize valedictorians and salutatorians? The answer, they offer, is that it is good for everyone's self-esteem. (Even the would-be valedictorian?)

The movement to eliminate competitive rankings in American schools has made great headway in recent years. Pat Riordan, dean of admissions at George Mason University, researched class rankings for the National Association of Secondary Schools. She estimates that 60 percent of schools no longer use them. At Community High, a public secondary school in Ann Arbor, Michigan, academic awards at graduation are kept a secret. There are no class rankings, no valedictorian. At graduation, everyone gets a turn to speak. As the guidance counselor explains, 'Everybody is seen as an equal contributor to the class of '99.'

WE HONOR ALL STUDENTS says a bumper sticker from Drew Elementary School in Arlington, Virginia. The implication is that schools with honor rolls dishonor those who do not qualify. Jim Mitchell, executive director of the Maryland Association of Elementary School Principals, explains the new hostility to the honor roll: 'It flies in the face of the philosophy of not making it so competitive for those little kids…We even frown on spelling bees.[11]

Understand me, children's emotional and behavioral displays or problems should not be ignored. However, The problem arises, in Robyn M. Dawes' opinion, when teachers assume that in their role of counselor they must help to establish a child's self-esteem *prior* to teaching the child anything. He says:

> But if self-esteem (academic self-esteem, anyway) primarily reflects achievement, and achievement results in large part from hard work, then such efforts are misdirected. Ironically, the results that the teachers attempt to achieve as counselors would be better achieved by abandoning that role and instead concentrating on teaching and insisting on standards of performance.[12]

Very unlike what is worded in our Declaration, Openness attempts to keep all people on an equal plane under the notion that all men **are** equal. It works at fulfilling this belief through its second strategy: lowering expectations. Opting to lower rather than to raise expectations makes things easier. More is rarely given when least is expected. This is neither isolated to the slothful (though the absence of incentives will likely produce laziness) nor to the dim-witted but also pertains to the indefatigable and formally educated person. Henry David Thoreau said, "Our life is frittered away by detail…simplify, simplify." I first heard of a similar perspective from my chemistry professor—and romantic alchemist—Dr. Paul C. McKinney, who on several occasions lectured that things were difficult enough already. He said chemists try to make the intricate and complex simpler because, after all, who wants to work hard?[iii]

Simplifying instructions to make the job more easily comprehended is not altogether the same as lowering the bar to make the job simpler. While opting to lower expectations increases the rate of successes—for now the unqualified (the slow, weak, inept, and otherwise disinterested) can perform up to par—it also, and more importantly, robs the element of

---

[iii] I credit my successful completion of chemistry to my good professors who taught jointly, bringing a humanities (liberal arts) flavor to the methodical and formulated science. As Ralph Waldo Emerson said, "The man who can make hard things easy is the educator."

challenge from those skilled and ahead of the game. Is the benefit of greater self-esteem and confidence among more students worth the cost of education mitigation? 'Sadder but wiser' was how Sigmund Freud ultimately believed the patient should leave therapy. This is not to suggest teachers should be callous. My classmates and I are not just bricks in the wall to be told what to think; we are people. And I think as such every professor should treat his students with encouragement and respect. Nonetheless, student self-esteem, it seems to me, ought not dictate the curriculum or pace of instruction. I am not assuming a mere two or three pupil are prodigious and their advanced genius crippled by the rest of the school. No, the case needn't be that hyperbolic. A good handful of students find themselves in the constant association of classmates less determined, less motivated and passionate, and less intelligent or equipped for the course. But here is the problem: suddenly the first group of students—the competent, productive students—find themselves acing what was expected to be a rigorous course. Why?

The potential danger in the present scenario is a deterioration of good study habits because, again, rarely is more given when least is expected. The attitude of 'I don't have to prepare, I don't have to study' is encouraged with each menial assignment. True, there is the real possibility of the work ethic or smartness (for lack of a better term) of the top students somehow rubbing off on the lesser-inclined and equipped ones. The hope, I imagine, was for the latter to model the former. In our Western culture, however, it ought to be recognized that the still prevailing stalwart of individualism may impede the humility to follow and model others even at the detriment of personal success. With everyone being primed for 'leadership' who is left to do the following? The sheer economics of organization demands some lead and some follow. But modern education is so hip to cooperative-learning, leaving everyone to be his own captain, to follow no one, that too many students are dubbed into thinking themselves leaders when they no little about leadership. (How can they when they model—look to—no one?) What they mistake for leadership or independence is really more in the light of nonconformity, which is not all-together the same thing.

What happens to the better minds in modern universities, to the students of above average intelligence whom are actually eager to learn? The answer, according to Ayn Rand is that "what they find and have to endure is a long, slow process of psycho-epistemological torture."[13] How may have the American education system gotten to this point? One sign points toward public education—the very notion of it. Some people interpret governmentally funded schools and programs unjust in nature. The rationale is that the law in taking from some people "enough to pay the teachers who are appointed by government to instruct others without charge"[14] commits a violation of liberty and property. I do not accept this. The logic is much too cerebral, absent of humanity, and seems to excuse government's obligation to its citizens. I cannot tear down the soundness of the argument anymore than I can ever convince a student of chemistry in the real science-ness of psychology, but since I refuse to accept their rationalization, believing public schooling can be worth its salt[iv], I therefore must regard public education (along with the social welfare system, though not necessarily the one we have at present) as a necessary evil.

I rest my rejection on this cornerstone: it is in the best interests of the State to educate its citizens if it is to be warranted the world over as a civilized society. Roscoe Pound contended "one of the major functions of civilization is the raising of human powers to their highest possible unfolding, of the maximum of human control over external nature and over internal nature." [15]

It is a common misconception that equal opportunities means equal chances. Are all racers equally qualified to reach the finish line just because they commence running on the same mark? Of course not. The various

---

[iv] I cannot legitimately argue, not even theoretically, for the abolition of public schooling. I am a product of the public school system and am now attending a private college. If memory serves me correct it was not the public schooling that was a disservice. It was some of the politics, I mean, people running it.

determinants include among other things, the number of hours practiced, quality of the practice, rate of equipment, diet, sufficient rest, physical condition, experience, and the will to win. What the provision of opportunities does is to lubricate the tight hold of aristocracies on formal schooling. The impenetrable class system is now made permeable, as the success of the learned is not exclusive to the rich and elite. Public education is essential for a democratic regime to ensure its power and status in the continuing years even if the means to this end result in taxes to provide for the campus and staff.

The twofold problem with modern public education, as I see it, is first, public schools must accept everyone and second, education in opposition to the standing regime. Because they operate on property taxes and government capital, generally public schools do not have the privilege of selecting who will and who wont 'learn' within their walls. The doors must be open to all, including riff-raff, trouble-makers, pregnant students, atheists, anarchists, and the bothersome rest who can collectively be tagged (apparently) uneducable. Besides the low degree of selective-ness, it is another problem all together when the educational system lags in its moral goal to teach on ethics, citizenship, and about the presiding government. From Allan Bloom: Always important is the political regime, which needs citizens who are in accord with its fundamental principle. "Aristocracies want gentlemen, oligarchies men who respect and pursue money, and democracies lovers of equality."

A very good model of structured public education in the Western world can be observed in England.[v] The children, rich and poor, are sent off to

---

[v] In Great Britain, single-sex classrooms are being experimented and reinstituted to address the widening academic gap between boys and girls. According to Christina Sommers (*The War Against Boys*, 2000), "Many British educational leaders believe that the modern classroom fails boys by being too unstructured, too permissive, and too hostile to the spirit of competition that so often provides boys with the incentive to learn and excel...By contrast, the looming prospect of an underclass of...barely literate American boys has yet to become a cause for open concern among American educators..."(160).

school where they sport school uniforms and learn the rules of being a good citizen, i.e., a gentleman or lady, in addition to general studies of reading, writing, rhetoric, and geography. Whereas the English transaction of teaching-and-learning-produces a noticeable learned accent from say cockney, the American system entertains the significance of Ebonics.

Another possible explanation for the pattern of lowering versus raising expectations might have something to do with the commonness of public education. It is the law that children receive schooling until their late teens where they have the option of legally dropping out. Gone is the unlocking power of the high school degree which is soon to be joined in step by the bachelors (of arts) degree—from all but the most committed and reputable institutions, that is. Like a machine mass producing products versus handmade items so too does the quality of education shine less brightly among crowded schools versus private or even home schooling. This is a virtual truism. I am not arguing good students and teachers cannot be found in public or state schools or that bad students and cynical pedagogues cannot be found in private academies. What I think has happened is a general lack of appreciation for education because the transaction is so common today. Modern students do not appreciate schooling in the same vein as their grandparents. The bottom line is that making school easier through lowered expectations will not help matters because it will not raise interest and esteem in learning.

Sometimes easier is not always better. For example, movie buffs do not like it when the plot and outcome are banal and too predictable. Video game enthusiasts quickly tire of beating the first 20 levels to save the world from the evil neo-Axis powers. Serious students typically hate classes when the teacher has to repeatedly slow down to keep the other students up to pace. Even young readers come to learn that easy picture books are for babies. They would rather have a 'regular' book, please.

Lowering expectations takes the beauty—the challenge—of the task from the people capable and willing to tackle it. What's worse, it sends the message *Don't strive (i.e., use your inherited or learned advantages) because you will get no more and no less than the bump on the log standing beside you.* And you thought Kansas sent a blow to Darwinism. Muhammad Ali said, "What keeps me going is goals." Without high expectations there is little incentive to do your best. There are no goals to keep you going.

Next, standards are threatened by catering to the lowest common denominator. Catering to the lowest common denominator guarantees a bigger turnout, a bigger market. But sometimes bigger is not always better. Unfortunately, socially speaking, the lowest common denominator is very rarely the opposite of cheap, sleazy, easy, or entertaining. We are living in a time in which all public discourse becomes a form of entertainment. Being probably the biggest perpetrators of pandering to the lowest common denominator, the broadcast media are a good metaphor of Openness.

Like Openness advocates, TV executives zero in on the lowest common denominator. What does Openness do to make sure everyone passes? It lowers expectations. What do the far majority of television programs do to garner large ratings? They lower sophistication. It is not hard to see why pure educational channels like the Public Broadcasting Station (PBS) is largely funded by private donations. The vast viewing audience does not particularly care for 'education' outside of the school building and likely does not have the attention span for it. Television producers know this, which helps explain why visual interest is their paramount objective. Their bread and butter come from those who don't listen to unsponsored programs.[16] The average length of a shot on a network program is about 3.5 seconds.[17] Television is not bad—the causes and effects simply happen to be the nature of the beast as much as getting wet is the result of going swimming. The medium "must **suppress the content** of ideas in order to **accommodate** the requirements of visual interest," writes Neil Postman, author of *Amusing Ourselves to Death*, "that is to say, to accommodate the values of show business [underscore added]."[18] An avid watcher of television I do not think television, itself, is bad but its armory of illusion and pillbox of insight justifies Socratism's inference of the "essential perversity and reprehensibility of what exists."[19] I have read that George Bernard Shaw, upon seeing the bedazzling neon lights of Broadway and 42 Street for the first time, remarked how beautiful it must be if you cannot read.

Sitcoms and television dramas have experienced an influx in sex (not love) scenes, openly decadent characters, and dialogue over masturbation, doing "it" for the first time, orgasms, safe sex, teen sex, and male impotence. We've come a long way from Mr. and Mrs. Brady sharing the same bed. Sometimes the situations employ double entendres and other times they just say it like it is. Sex sells, goes the mantra. But that is no profound revelation! Being one of the most intimate, hallowed, anticipated, and vital behaviors for our existence, it should come as little surprise that sex sells. TV also airs a lot of senseless violence and not just between cops and robbers (that's old hat) but also between spouses, lawless citizens (apparently in a city experiencing a police strike) and young people...very young people. And the televised hour of such material is inconsequential; prime time or no prime time, it is there.

The news media has a saying: *If it bleeds, it leads.* To put it less colorfully, if the news item can be framed for our amusement, then it gets airtime. Despite the consensus that daily news shows only report bad news, Postman believes it is for this very same reason that viewers are urged to "tune in tomorrow." "What for?" he asks. "One would think that several minutes of murder and mayhem would suffice as material for a month of sleepless nights."[20] He goes on to explain that we loyally join our favorite anchor crew night after night because it is regarded as break time, fun time; "we know that the 'news' is not to be taken seriously."[21]

Yet, surely in this physically vast world there are other topics that greatly interest viewers. Can not TV offer something more sophisticated than sex, sex, sex, and guns, guns, guns to a literate and civilized society? But I suppose the social and intellectual environment that created television is irreversible. So long as explicit sex and violence turn viewers on, which translates into high ratings, the medium will continue to broadcast more sex and violence. The subject matter will become increasingly pervasive and gratuitous.[vi]

Before proceeding to the fourth manner in which standards are threatened by Openness, I think here begs the question, Why have standards declined and how does Openness and television contribute to it? And why is there an abundance of short attention span sufferers? Assuming this was not always the case, when (and why) did the change occur? Christina Sommers points to Rousseaunian principles that replaced directed learning sometime around the 1960s. With this change came a focus on self-esteem and student creativity over teacher led curriculum and rote learning. Writer and social critic Marshall McLuhan believed people's lives are changed by the media. He labeled it information technological determinism, meaning each change in information technology creates corresponding social, economic, political, and psychological changes. He outlined it as such: the current electronic age was preceded by the printing press, preceded by a time of communication symbols, preceded by the pre-literate or oral society. Each new medium of communication can safely be said to recreate the existing discourse. This is what he meant when he said that the medium is the message.

[vi] It would be intriguing to analyze this along Daryl Bem's "exotic becomes erotic" model (1996). Though Bem invented the phrase in his study on sexual orientation, the theory can be applied to other contexts. Understanding the theory, if the *other* becomes so common that it no longer is seen as different, mysterious, rebellious—exotic—then it presumably will cease to be erotic and sought after (Barlow/Durand text, 303). For the purpose of this essay, the concern is wether the emotional gratification will eventually reach a plateau where television's special effects and graphic content no longer excite the large viewership, resulting in big ratings.

In *Closing*, the author wrote that making sex so accessible and easy actually "trivialize, de-eroticize, and demystify sexual relations"(100). It is generally well known that veteran players in the adult entertainment industry tend to become apathetic, cynical, emotionless, and burned out about their profession and life. Will the same mentality arrest television watchers? Only time will tell. Stay tuned.

For our purposes, we examine the transition from the printing press to the electronic age. Neil Postman, a close student of McLuhan, expounds on the effects of television. In *Amusing Ourselves to Death,* Postman regards the shift from the "Age of Typography" to the "Age of Television" as "the most significant American cultural fact of the second half of the twentieth century."[22] As we move from one medium to another, all content will need to be reported and recast in a format more appropriate to the approaching medium.

While citing a few exceptions, his general stance is that television is more show business and less substance. His contempt for television is analogous to Socrates' for tragic art. The modern student might be surprised to learn that Socrates refrained from attending tragedies because he opposed tragic art and was so cerebral (Socratic) that it took lonely jail confinement for him to finally recognize and acknowledge the usefulness of music and poetry. So you see, not even the best were indiscriminate in their tastes. But I digress. Listen to Friedrich Nietzsche's explanation of the Socratic attitude toward fine arts:

> Let us imagine the one great Cyclops eye of Socrates fixed on tragedy, an eye in which the fair frenzy of artistic enthusiasm had never glowed...[it saw] something rather unreasonable, full of clauses apparently without effects, and effects apparently without causes; the whole, moreover, so motley and dangerous tinder for sensitive and susceptible souls...But to Socrates it seemed that tragic art did not even 'tell the truth'; moreover, it addressed itself to 'those who are not very bright,' not to the philosopher: a twofold reason for shunning it. Like Plato, he reckoned it among the flattering arts which portray only the agreeable, not the useful.[23]

Postman does not regard television as an extension of the printing press: "Television does not extend or amplify literate culture. It attacks it."[24]

He contends that the change affected by the advent of television made every avenue—politics, sports, religion, education—a distributor of entertainment. Thus, the problem is not so much that television presents us with entertaining subject matter in as much as it presents all subject matter as entertaining, "which is another issue altogether." We are conditioned to 15-second commercial sound bytes and flashing pictures. Everything just rubs the surface. There is no depth. Why read a book when you can go see it at the movies? Better still, why bother with movie lines and people when you can download or simply surf the Web at the click of a mouse?

Just as typography once dictated the form of conducting such things as education, politics, and business, Postman sees television taking command. Writing at the dawn of the twenty-first century, I see the Internet fiercely vying for that position. The moral of the story is nicely summed by a social critic: "Television offers viewers a variety of subject matter, requires minimal skills to comprehend it, and is largely aimed at emotional gratification."[25] The broadcast media cater to the lowest common denominator.

Fourthly, exercising more tolerance and less chastisement threatens standards. When we condone wrongdoing then we have done ourselves a great disfavor. In recent decades there has been trumpeted more tolerance for this and more tolerance for that.

Tolerance is a good attribute—a humane quality—but it cannot be so freely granted at every faulty turn. It must be allotted in moderation. There are times when chastisement is very appropriate and the absence of it inappropriate. To abandon punishment for fear of being perceived tyrannical or politically incorrect is unfortunate. It is unfortunate because it sends the message that nothing wrong or improper was done.

For instance, children will test boundaries to see how far they can proceed. It is natural. It is part of the learning and exploring process. If the child breaks a rule—perhaps mimicking something seen on TV or picked up at a friend's house or on the playground—and the parent spares discipline, then the child interprets such behavior acceptable. The child reasons—logically so—that he has done nothing improper or bad. Consequently the standard of behavior is more likely to fall than rise.

Standards exist to give us something to live by, a measurement, if you will. With standards we have a gauge of normalcy and achievement. Albeit some believe rules are meant to be broken, the justice system should not burn law books any more than a sensible person should do away with insurance simply because there exist scam artists. Such thinking is cynical and unreasonable. Besides, if there were no rules, then malefactors and delinquents would be hard pressed to find something to break![vii] Similarly, the institution of marriage ought not be dismissed just because many people have babies out of wedlock. The idea is **not** to have children out of wedlock, especially if the parents are themselves children. Yet, it happens and families manage to deal with it all right. But, how many can undoubtedly say it was planned? The point is, minus standards far too many would not know right from wrong. Wrong might be committed—sure—but as the saying goes *you can send a kid off to college but you can't make him think.*

Too much tolerance, while well intended, defeats the purpose of standards and moral instruction. Here is some practical advice: stop trying to *understand* every lapse and insubordination. Do something about it so the individual might *understand* his lapse or insubordination. Chastisement is not a bad thing and it does not make the user a mean person. Appropriate discipline—authoritative discipline—signals a transgression. Discipline should never be discarded. Mistakes, the ingredients of experience, are steps toward progress. Learning from our mistakes makes us wiser because we now know what not to do and, more importantly, why not to do it. More, learning from other people's mistakes is even better—you can't make them all yourself.

[vii] An individual's search for something to rebel against might, in reality, be a cry for help from themselves and from one another.

Openness is preoccupied with not hurting feelings, afraid of being a meanie. Since it does not want to be authoritarian (because it challenges authority) it accepts all transgressions save the man who is not open to everything. Not even God (in any religion) accepts all transgressions. He knows all. He blesses and forgives. And when bad goes to worst, He permits the little incorrigible to Hell. As someone, I know not who, once nicely put it, "Society needs to condemn a little more and understand a little less."

[9] From *The Norton Anthology of American Literature,* Shorter 5th edition, (New York: W.W.Norton & Co., 1999), 325.

[10] *The Law,* 1.

[11] Christina Hoff Sommers, *The War Against Boys,* (New York: Simon & Schuster, 2000), 169. See also June Kronholz, "At Many U.S. Schools, the Valedictorian Is Now a Tricky Issue," *Wall Street Journal,* (May 17, 1999): 1; Ann O'Hanlon, "Ruckus Over the Honor Roll," *Washington Post,* (April 8, 1997): D1.

[12] Robyn M. Dawes, *House of Cards: Psychology and Psychotherapy Built on Myth,* (New York, New York, The Free Press, 1994), 248.

[13] *The New Left,* 31.

[14] *The Law,* 28.

[15] This was one element of five jural postulates Roscoe Pound outlined law should affect for the maintenance of a civilized society in *Social Control Through Law,* 1942, 132, quoted by Edward B. McLean, *Law and Civilization: The Legal Thought of Roscoe Pound,* (Lanham, Maryland: University Press of America, 1992), 221.

[16] *All About Eve,* prod., Darryl F. Zanuck and dir. Joseph L. Mankiewicz, 138 mins., 20th Century Fox, 1950, film.

[17] Neil Postman, *Amusing Ourselves To Death: Public Discourse in the Age of Show Business,* (New York: Penguin Books, 1986),86.

[18] Ibid., 92.

[19] *Tragedy,* section 13, 87.

[20] Ibid, 87.

[21] Crompton, 87.

[22] *Amusing Ourselves,* 8.

[23] *Tragedy,* section 14, 89-90.

[24] *Amusing Ourselves,* 84.

[25] Ibid, 86.

THE UNITED FISHBOWLS
OF AMERICA

▼────

Big Brother is watching you

—"Nineteen-Eightyfour" by George Orwell

THREAT TO PRIVACY

Privacy means closed and our dear philosophy means un-closed. Privacy is the prey and Openness is the predator.

By privacy I mean personal space. When personal space is threatened, conflict usually ensues. We are losing boundaries of privacy. Because Openness is being strongly stressed in and for every facet of our daily lives everything is becoming visible; everything needs to be observed. Is America becoming a nation of voyeurs? Let us examine the consequences of dissolving the partition betwixt public and private. When the people accept transparency and visibility as important social values at large, then they are living in a self-imposed prison and not an open society.[26] Two mechanisms accountable for our eroding privacy, innocence, and reservation are television and multiculturalism.

Since the advent of television, America has quickly become an entertainment society. Many Americans welcomed the medium into their homes: first, in the living room or basement and now almost every household has (at least) one in the bedroom and kitchen. Throughout its short history TV has managed to reverse the roles, bringing viewers into the tube instead of viewers bringing it into the home. TV's reversal of fortune reminds me of George Herbert's insightful poem "Avarice" in which the tool becomes the owner and the owner the tool. I refer the reader to it. In America, television has become more of a medium and less of a technology.[27] "A technology, in other words, is merely a machine," explained Postman. "A medium is the social and intellectual environment a machine creates."[28]

Cable TV, always a bit more edgy, has shows like "Taxicab Confessions"[viii], "Real Sex", and several specialized channels. (There is even a channel that televises real life surgical operations and another that airs nothing but cartoons 24 hours everyday.) Network television has not shied away from what is called "reality TV." Since the late eighties, 'reality' shows like "Cops" and "Home Video of Deadliest this and Funniest that" have crowded networks' lineups.

Look! Real policemen actually chasing drug dealers and abusive dads down alleyways, over fences, under bridges, across an intersection, into crawl spaces, through a tunnel, and onto the hood of a rusty Sedan where the bad guy is finally apprehended and read his Miranda rights. Who knew that a TV camera could do all that without the (presumed guilty) suspect seeing him coming up the block? Give that cameraman a Pulitzer! And give the drug dealer a Darwin Award for being stupid enough to ignore approaching policemen and camera crew.

[viii] "Taxicab Confessions" is a cable series about real cab passengers' conversations and behaviors being caught on tape by a hidden camera. The driver knows the camera is there but not the customer. Some episodes have exposed people babbling about their miserable lives or having sex or getting stoned, or just sharing thoughts they otherwise might not have were they aware a camera was recording them. Each episode ends with the famous candid camera debriefing. Everyone shares a big laugh. After all, it is not everyday you get to be on television and fifteen minutes (in a cab) is so fleeting.

So successful has this trend proven itself that it has been taken to the next (unbelievable) level—televising ordinary people for television's sake. The popularity of these shows (e.g., *The Real World, Survivor, Who Wants to Marry a Multi-Millionaire?, Blind Date* (imagine actually going on a real blind date with a camera crew in tow!)) highlight, if nothing else, that people like to watch...and to be watched. Hence, the rise of voyeur television or vtv, for short. On one side of the tube millions of viewers loyally tune in to gorge on the drama and humiliation of the "characters" while the viewees live for the cameras; playing, eating, sleeping, bickering, sexing, working, and bitching at each other...all for the worth of being watched by millions of hungry eyes.

Like something out of the movies (e.g., *The Truman Show* and *Ed TV*) Americans really dig looking in on the lives of each other. According to a Time/CNN telephone poll, when asked whether reality-based shows were a disturbing trend for society or just harmless entertainment, 59 percent of polled Americans regarded the shows as just entertainment. From the *Times* ("Voyeur TV: We like to watch")

> Ironically, the mainstream embrace of voyeurism comes precisely as many Americans feel their own privacy is in danger, be it from surveillance on the job, marketers on the Net or database-wielding bureaucrats in their HMOS.[29]

How can this be among a people so defensive of their privacy?[ix] Sounding a lot like Neal Postman, Neal Gabler, author of *Life the Movie: How Entertainment Conquered Reality* said in *Time* magazine, "Reality has become the greatest entertainment of all. It's symptomatic of a larger phenomenon that all of life is entertainment."[30] Now, CBS has launched *Big Brother*—of all the names in the world—in which ten people are

---

[ix] Ironically, it was during the Great Depression that the ever popular boardgame "Monopoly" caught on in America as did the notion of optimism (read Norman Vincent Peale's *The Power of Positive Thinking*).

locked inside a specially constructed house lined with cameras in every room (yes, even in *that* room). A 24-hr. website will enable die-hard voyeurs to hardly miss a moment. Other than narcissism and an apparent incomprehension of the severity of ominous surveillance what could possess people to hock all privacy, all respite? And of all things, for the amusement of others?

An even more telling example of the pervading medium and our obsession with it is the talk show war. Take your pick: Jerry Springer, Ricki Lake, Sally Jesse Raphael, Montel, Geraldo, MTV's Loveline, Maury Povich, and a slew of two-bit has-beens who didn't survive two seasons. These "talk" shows pimp the private issues of people. They exploit serious problems and, then, allow audience members turned psychologists to berate the panel. The formats operate on two goals: one, entertainment and two, problem-solving. (Regarding treatment, the validity of nationally televised humiliation that comes when a man confesses to another man that he has a crush on him or when women tell their lovers they moonlight as escorts or, worse, are biologically men, is still iffy).

The format of "talk" shows encourages the guests to air their dirty laundry on national television. (I insist on using quotations because amidst all the screaming, cussing, and crying, who is doing any of the talking?). The message is simple: be open, very open. Privacy? Well, just how do you suppose we solve your issues if you don't open up in front of a jeering bunch of strangers and television cameras, huh, huh? Openness, akin to the likes of Jerry Springer (and Internet perverts who operate voyeurism sites), wants us to believe that closure is an unhealthy thing of the past. Yet, whether they accept it or not, privacy is not analogous with repression. No one is likely to have an ulcer or go mad if he or she does not let the town and nation know about a marital tiff, or secret fantasy, or problem child, or fetish, or whatever. The danger in television is not that it is a source of amusement but rather that it represents everything as entertaining as if entertainment is the "natural format."

No where is the reversal of power more evident than parents petitioning government to help control what is viewed in their household. The admission, I can't possibly control what my child watches—even if I monitor the family room she'll just go watch TV in her bedroom—speaks loads of the times. Man can design and install the machine yet forget how to change channels from disagreeable programming or simply turn it off. What is to be said of a nation in which parents feel powerless to a common home appliance? Is it safe to say the hand that rules the remote control rules the home? How did television become the owner and not the tool? (It was intriguing and novel and it provides constant entertainment.) Why do people feel powerless to control it in their home? (They are beguiled by the stimulation it supplies. It provides an automatic refuge.) What keeps them from turning it off? (The fear of missing something.) All in all, despite the consensus that network television is explicit and offensive it is probably for this very reason that viewers loyally tune in to their favorite shows. Inappropriate material is couched in entertainment and at this point we may be too conditioned to the medium to directly do anything about it. Therefore 'concerned' groups look to the law to monitor what they may view on television.

Now someone will chime, "You yourself are doing this very same thing." Perhaps. But I act in a very different sense. Any similarity betwixt my argument and the campaign of TV reformers is the common enemy Openness which would have us believe explicitness is relative. There ends the commonality. I do not regard the television as the mistress regards her nanny, that is, a necessity. My contention is not over the introductory warnings of viewer discretion, but, rather, the prevalence of indiscretion (Openness) among network shows, not only making 'warnings' so commonplace as to render them insulting or infantile, but in many ways making it increasingly difficult to watch something clean, decent, and happy that needs no preface for viewer discretion. My attitude towards television is that it is only one of among several sources of information and entertainment; and probably the least substantial at that. I accept and recognize the power of television. It is the super surveillance and viewers' fascination with it I do not accept.

I maintain that candidness outside of the therapist's room especially on national television is not the best way to help problems. It embarrasses people and markets that embarrassment as entertainment for the world.[x] The whole genre of voyeurism television reeks Orwell and *Network*. A hefty price will be paid for living in a fish bowl.

Multiculturalists are also challenging our sense of privacy. Ethical diversity is by no means a bad thing. Our country is a conglomerate of immigrants, ethnicities, colors, and cultures. America has been called a great melting pot, a salad, and a stitched quilt. Each metaphor—a quilt, garden salad, melting pot—denotes the importance of the parts of the sum. For the past three decades multiculturalism has been heavily encouraged to combat the pathetic ignorance, which sometimes results from our differences; our different color, our different accents, our different cultures. The idea is that working together, playing together, going to school together will presumably show us how similar we really are and the beauty and significance in our cultural differences all the same. This is a noble venture, reader.

The problem of modern multiculturalists, so far as privacy is involved, is that they paradoxically maintain they are "color-blind" and that we are all the same while continuously working to identify and classify persons by categories. One is either this or that, or a third of this and the rest of that. If we are the same, then what need have we of a political correctness

---

[x] I think it a pretty sound assessment to say that Openness has gone too far when the graphics of the U.S. President's sexual activity are publicized and televised. The Monica Lewinsky scandal highlighted among other things the following two issues. First, the disrespect or mis-concept of the private and the personal. "The feminist slogan 'The personal is political'," writes Daphne Patai, "has transmuted into its opposite, 'The political is personal', which in turn has come to mean that where everything is political, nothing is." Secondly, a blow was sent to the feminist dogma of phallus dominance as a "major redistribution of 'power' had taken place."

nomenclature? Let us consider a quotation from Plato on this subject of diversification for oneness: "If you hold fast to this principle of avoiding contention over names you will turn out to be rich with an ever greater store of wisdom as you approach old age."[31]

One particular side effect has many Whites feeling pressured to befriend their minority counterparts. Commonly called 'white man's burden' or in social psychological terms, 'reverse discrimination' the result has some white people 'working' to get to know *everything* about their minority friend (because friends share feelings and things!) in order to fully understand their minority friend's oppression, world outlook, likes and dislikes, and such. Rogers and Prentice-Dunn (1981) investigated the behavior—phenomenon?—once commonly termed 'regressive racism.' Their experiments indicated that when anger was aroused with interracial behavior the displayed contemporary egalitarian norms gave way to the "old historic pattern of racial discrimination."

Reverse discrimination, said the psychologists, is the overt manifestation of white people's viewing themselves as egalitarian and feeling threatened by the prospect of appearing prejudiced (for a fuller body of the quotation see the footnote).[xi] They want to be able to sincerely say, "Some of my closest friends are Black." Every time I hear

---

[xi] Reverse discrimination is the overt manifestation of white people's viewing themselves as egalitarian and feeling threatened by the prospect of appearing prejudiced. Blacks would not be expected to display reverse discrimination, and studies of blacks' aggression have confirmed they do not (Wilson and Rogers, 1975). Both blacks' and whites' behavior, however, can be traced to the same underlying source: Both races seem to be 'reacting against the older, traditional patterns for their races' (Griffin and Rogers, 1977, p. 157).

This new norm [egalitarian] is especially prevalent among college students. Surveys at the university where the present study was conducted confirmed that the current norm among white students is an unprejudiced, egalitarian view of the races…Theoretically, reverse discrimination is a product of this relatively new egalitarian view of blacks (Dutton, 1976).

that statement or something to that effect, I think to myself, is this white guy serious or what?

There is a flip side to the coin: minorities (and who isn't one these days[xii]) do not want to live under a microscope. I am Black—and proud—so what? As a Black person I realize I am an African-American, a name that pays homage to my lost ancestry while acknowledging my allegiance and citizenship to the U.S.[xiii] One should not feel impressed to know everything about me in the ridiculous attempt to know what Black people think. I am a person, not a cultural resume. Openness it appears to me has disillusioned folks into assuming so much is extra special about minorities that the person who does not particularly stress multiculturalism is not only committing a big disservice but probably a racial one at that. "Nonetheless, I'm sick of diversity," admits Roger Clegg, general counsel of the Center for Equal Opportunity, in Washington. "The opposite of being pro-diversity is not being anti-diversity. It's being diversity-indifferent, and that's me. My T-shirt would not say 'Diversity Sucks.' It would say 'Diversity—Who Cares?'" His argument is that diversity proponents have tired their contradictory claims, misusing and manipulating aims toward unity. An America that is multiracial and multiethnic, yes, contends Clegg, Mutlicultural, no. "*E pluribus unum*: Out of many, one."[32]

[xii] Long after this particular essay was penned I happened upon C-Span television and recognized the speaker as former KKK Grand Wizard and presidential candidate David Duke. He was speaking before a supportive bunch in favor of European-American rights.

[xiii] One of the earliest figures I recall using the term African-American was Malcolm X (post-pilgrimage) who, during his childhood, was impacted by his father's involvement in Marcus Garvey's Back to Africa Movement. The term did not result from political dissention. It was not a means to be politically correct. Rather, African-American was the result of a cultural awakening from an identity crisis circa Black Power Movement. Unlike for other minorities, there is no corresponding country for black people to go to, that is to say, there is no Blackland. From an effort to remedy a people from this lack of cultural identity—destroyed by the "peculiar institution"—the dualism of the black citizen is captured in African-American.

For one, I think 'multicultural' minded liberals with their deluge of questions about your background, about what [your people] like to dance to, wear, cook, watch on TV, et cetera, et cetera, et cetera, are annoying. A conversation of questions is an interview in disguise. Why do they feel compelled to do this? They say it is because they want to understand us. Because they are our friends and friends are open to one another, they say. Yet, I say, befriend me as a friend, not as a squishy liberal or anthropologist. Conversely the teething conservatives about campus mistake tokenism for multiculturalism. Unlike their political counterparts, they befriend you because you stand a part from the rest of 'your kind'; you already seem 'like one of them.' 'Twixt the difference between the college liberals and the college conservatives? The former look at how alike our differences are and call it diversity, the latter look at how different our like-nesses are and call it diversity.

[26] Daphne Patai, *Heterophobia: Sexual Harassment and the Future of Feminism,* (Lanham: Rowman & Littlefield Publishers, Inc., 1998), 199.

[27] *Amusing Ourselves,*85.

[28] Ibid., 84.

[29] James Poniewozik. "We like to watch," *Time,* 26 June 2000, 61.

[30] Ibid.

[31] Plato, *Statesman,*trans. J. B. Skemp, ed. Martin Ostwald (New York: Liberal Arts Press, 1957), 261e.

[32] Roger Clegg, "Why I'm Sick of the Praise for Diversity on Campuses," *The Chronicle of Higher Education,* July 14, 2000, B8.

The Intangibles
▼

Trust thyself: every heart vibrates to that iron string

—Ralph Waldo Emerson

I can't stand squishy liberals!

—Anonymous schoolmate

Threat to Conviction and Honesty

One would be hard pressed to get an honest, thoughtful response from ordinary people nowadays. Openness has so pervaded our way of life that it has threatened conviction and honesty. How, you ask? For the moment, suffice it to say through the stressing of relativism. All too often in class discussion I hear what seems to me whitewashed, insincere, PC statements and sycophantic questions. Much of the dialogue not only caters to the professors' egos, but also has this surreal hallmarkish quality to them, almost as if a professional speechwriter scripted it. Sometimes (thinking out loud) I ask, Are these guys serious? Really, since when did you support that idea? For instance, a classmate might 'passionately' agree with the professor that the college needs to "get with it" and go coeducational so that we might learn (?) how to interact with females in the "real world"

(?), when only of all the semesters I have known him he has supported traditional single-sex education.

It is adulterated fluff like this that really makes attending classes sometimes unbearable. I imagine such would be the case for any student who wants to take his work seriously. I think to myself, This is pathetic. Why am I wasting life sitting here? It is a "long, slow process of psycho-epistemological torture." Certainly, language and attitudes have to remain in check, but for the love of conviction, "if you would be a man, speak what you think to-day in words as hard as cannon balls, and to-morrow speak what to-morrow thinks in hard words again, though it contradict everything you said to-day."[33] One of the best pieces of advice I ever took was, I confess, gathered from one of those posters covered with quotations and dull cliches. It said: "Don't talk; say something." For, as Benjamin Franklin wisely expresses, "Speak not but what may benefit others or yourself. Avoiding trifling Conversation."[xiv]

Oddly enough, instead of causing discussion to be open, and perhaps unsuitably colorful, the relativism of Openness has caused the dialogue to be feigned and self-monitored. It seems to have scared people into being so tolerable that they accept—more accurately, claim to accept—all things including those which clearly conflict with their beliefs, character, upbringing, and better judgement. Why is this? "The students, of course, cannot defend their opinion," argues Mr. Bloom. "It is something with which they have been indoctrinated. The best they can do is point out all the opinions and cultures there are and have been."[34] In other words, because Openness advances tolerance over chastisement and acceptance over tolerance it has influenced a generation of American minds into

---

[xiv] This was on Silence, the second of his thirteen self-ascribed virtues. He writes in The Autobiography [Part Two], "…my Desire being to gain Knowledge…and considering that in Conversation it was obtain'd rather by the Use of the Ears than of the Tongue, and therefore wishing to break a Habit I was getting into of Prattling, Punning and Joking, which only made me acceptable to trifling Company, I gave Silence the second Place."

thinking that unconditional acceptance is the hallmark of compassion and humanity, that all things are, in fact, relative.

Not only is there an uncommitted or surreal (and sometimes cynical) element to current American academics but there is also an absence of reason and practicality. Are we to perceive this direction of America's education system is producing just and knowledgeable citizens for a stronger democratic society? The future of a nation cannot be better off in the hands of young minds impressed with beliefs that reality is a meaningless term, obfuscation is the mark of philosophy, acceptance is the mark of compassion, "and, above all, the hallmark of an intellectual is the denial of the intellect."[35]

What are we to make of professional academia? Ayn Rand had this to say of her academic colleagues:

> When and if academic commentators gave any thought to the practical results of their theories, they were predominantly united in claiming that uncertainty and skepticism are socially valuable traits which would lead to tolerance of differences, flexibility, social 'adjustment' and willingness to compromise. Some went so far as to maintain explicitly that intellectual certainty is the mark of a dictatorial mentality, and that chronic *doubt*—the absence of firm convictions, the lack of absolutes—is the guarantee of a peaceful, 'democratic' society.
> They miscalculated.[36]

Critiquing the more current state of the curriculum, Allan Bloom suggested, "The point is to propagandize acceptance of different ways, and indifference to their real content is as good a means as any."[37]

One day in class the topic concerned anthropology (or 'the Other') as we had just read excerpts of Margaret Mead's work on the Samoans. The professor, in an effort to personalize the issue, directed the discussion to America's conflict with the present 'Other', Saddam Hussein and Iraq. He asked for our opinion regarding Hussein's regime. Amazingly the table was silent, not from deep thought but timidity. Finally a classmate inquisitively volunteered, "Well, we can't judge him. Who are we to criticize his leadership?" What! Like the professor, I was almost dumbfounded by the sentiment. Here we were talking about one of the most tyrannical, murderous, and oppressive U.S.-hating dictators still breathing and all the student could contribute was that the class might try understanding Saddam Hussein. Tell a tasteless (i.e., politically incorrect) joke and he's likely to file a complaint or lawsuit, but speak down a dictator and he wonders, "Why?"

My classmate miscalculated in what was an aim to "say the right thing" and probably stroke the professor's ego. This is just one of several instances where I have noticed peers either too ill-equipped or apprehensive to be honest in discussion. At least, I hope the student was not being serious. I like to think he was taking the easy way out by being indifferent instead of speaking accordingly.[xv] Indifference, after all, does not involve you taking sides thus removing the scholarly burden of having to defend your position and, above all, reject a different position. Still, what does this say about the direction of America's education?

What is it that is so appealing about indifference and a lack of honest conviction, save the wide open door it leaves to exit a debate? Another case in point: sometimes around the meal table the discourse turns to deeper issues other than the ESPN highlights blaring from the dining hall television (there is always a television nearby). As always the same handful of mates maintained that intellectual certainty on basically anything is evidence of narrow-mindedness. They characteristically carry on about one having "sold out," or having a dictatorial mentality if one firmly contends a stance (opposite theirs, of course). These students believe in compromises and deem it nothing less than bigotry to express an absolute, be it moral or otherwise. This stigma is the antagonist of firm convictions.

[xv] The precept of Benjamin Franklin's seventh virtue *Sincerity*: Use no hurtful Deceit. Think innocently and justly; and, if you speak; speak accordingly.

For dread of probably being (mis) labeled sexist, racist, chauvinist, narrow-minded, insensitive, or old fashioned many people are wary of being expressive even when asked for their opinion. One to the contrary is Dr. Laura Schlessinger, the sharp-tongued radio psychotherapist. Dr. Laura gives her listeners honest and unequivocal advice and she has come under fire for it. Gay activists charge her expression of her moral and religious standards slur their lifestyle. This is the price paid for not conforming to relativist Openness. How quickly the Left forget that freedom of speech is a) sometimes disagreeable, and b) not exclusively theirs.

In actuality, because so many people (not just undergraduates) are trying to be everything to everybody we might as well be at a costume gala for they all are wearing masks. There is no genuineness. Their irregular masks, like the chamber of infinite wisdom and eternal youth in *Gulliver's Travels*, keep them from seeing the myth that is a peaceful democratic society resulting from endless compromises and devout tolerance. Nietzsche said thus: your heroes, too, have only copied, masked passions and speak only copied, masked speeches."[38] In this land of the free and home of the brave how can it be anything but disturbing and disappointing that iconoclasts are successfully psyching out people from being 'brave' enough to freely contribute to discussion?

The glaring problem in being without convictions is the difficulty it poses in figuring out when and if someone is being honest. Straddling the fence, like the ideology itself, makes one unreliable. Who can tell when the person is supporting one thing and not the other? In effect, Openness recreates intangible people. People of intangibility cannot be grasped or adequately comprehended because they lack substance. They can not be 'figured out.' They are without substance because they have no convictions, no genuine calling. They lack sound convictions because they are too timid and weak to take a stand; but they cannot stand on an issue because they have no backbone—caustic slogans and bromides, yes, but no backbone. Thus, these human invertebrates, these advocates of Openness, remain squishy and intangible.

33 Ralph Waldo Emerson, *Self-Reliance* (1841).

34 *Closing,* 26.

35 *The New Left,* 26.

36 Ibid., 26-27.

37 *Closing,* .35.

38 *Tragedy,* section 10.

Why XY?

---------------▼---------------

"Girls will be boys and boys will be girls/ It's a mixed up place…"

—The Who

Anyone who wants a firsthand experience of male-averse attitudes and anti-boy rhetoric can get it anywhere the girl partisans gather. It is at their conferences that they are most uninhibitedly themselves.

—Christina Hoff Sommers

Threat to Masculinity

A huge voice of Openness is the modern feminist movement. The feminist movement, for all of its virtues and ideals, has the unfortunate side effect of emasculating maleness. I call it an unfortunate side effect because emasculation is not the purported aim of the feminist agenda. Those within the movement see themselves advancing and encouraging the potential of woman. In contrast, those outside of the movement are convinced of its aim to emotionally and psychologically castrate manhood. Perhaps the castration is not just one of psychology and emotion. Judging from a demonstration of feminists wielding open scissors in the V-shape for victory in celebration of John Wayne Bobbitt's severed penis, it is not erroneous to believe physical castration is meant as well. Careful ladies, you don't want to run with scissors. You may injure someone. I am taking careful consideration not to generalize as simply women's groups. I see the card-carrying feminist reformers as the specific culprit threatening maleness. Even here I regrettably must generalize feminists, as I understand there is an emerging spectrum of feminism. In America the breakdown is often equality versus superiority feminists. At fifth glance the two appear identical as all feminists speak about equality and seem to carry on with an air of superiority about them. During a lecture visit to my college Carol Tavris, social psychologist and feminist, highlighted people's recognition of various ways to be anything and everything—but a feminist. "There is supposed to be only one way to be a feminist."

The difference in the general breakdown I am told, though too subtle it may seem to some readers, is this: equality feminism, which Carol Tavris subscribes to, seeks to level the invoked discrepancies betwixt the sexes, acknowledging the virtues and shortcomings of both, and the significance of science. We should be open to identify change, said Tavris, when scientific data disconfirms our held beliefs. Superiority feminism advances the long renounced secret that women are superior to men and that it is only a matter of politics before equality rights the wrongs of misogyny and make a woman Commander in Chief, Chairwoman of the Joint Chiefs of Staff, Speaker of the House, the National Director of the Boys Scouts of America, and head of the Vatican. Perhaps no woman better articulated superiority feminism than Valerie Solanas with her S.C.U.M. Manifesto.

In her book, *Heterophobia: Sexual Harassment and the Future of Feminism,* Daphne Patai (who still considers herself a feminist) says, "Tolerance has never been a notable characteristic of feminism."[39] Failing to treat Lorena Bobbitt's butchery like the serious act it was merely boasters my claim of America's endangered maleness and a "manifestation of heterophobia."[40]

Evidence of this vicious side of Openness can be found in our changing lexicon, certain federal programs, the saliency of gay pride which was proceeded by the '70s "soft" male, and the deterioration of the traditional family nucleus. I will elaborate on each point.

Looking at our changing lexicon I have noticed the way of the word is unisex. More and more, the words *man* and *he* are being dropped from our daily vocabulary to be replaced by gender-blind terms. I can concede a rationale for changing some career related titles like stewardess and mailman, but others are ridiculous. 'Mankind', which we understand to mean those of man, i.e., humans (or more technically, **Homo-Sapiens**) is often replaced with 'humankind'—needlessly making the point that we are not all males. However, this is nothing entirely new. Traveling back to the 19th Century, we meet Mary Wollstonecraft, the first modern feminist. Wollstonecraft was a radical woman. For example, she refused to give up her last name and take that of her husband. (Incidentally the family name lives on through her only child who would also become prominent in her own right. The author of the classic novel, *The Monster of Dr. Frankenstein,* Mary Shelley Wollstonecraft better known simply as Mary Shelley.)

Of direct relevance to the issue at hand is Wollstonecraft's proposal for change as outlined in *The Vindication of the Rights of Woman.* In *Vindication*, she insists on the common utility of the words "human" and "humankind." In line with today's feminists, Wollstonecraft's argument is that "mankind" excludes women and, more directly, pertains to and concerns only men. According to the logic, *man* in the Biblical context is also sexist (or often misconstrued by clergymen to say the least) because it does not clearly refer to women. Hello, nor does the surface structure of Biblical *man* imply singularity. From context clues, we are able to understand Biblical "man's" connotations of plurality and generality.

Right now there is much fuss made over our English pronouns. The pronoun *he,* despite its encompassing feature of referring to both genders (and there are only two genders), it is commonly replaced with *he/she* even when no special distinction is being stressed. As an undergraduate student, I concede the benefits of using *he/she* to fatten reports and satisfy page requirements. I sometimes use same tactic even when speaking of one gender. For some reason the trick always passes the professors' critical read as they never mark against it. What does not go unmarked, however, is students' general employment of "he." At my college a few professors have made it a point to only use "She" in place of "he." Indoctrination of this sort deserves to be called out. In all seriousness this term—*he/she*—needlessly complicates the English vernacular. How queer it is to hear speakers say, "he slash she…" Give it time, *she/he* will eventually take the place of *he/she*.

Christina Hoff Sommers, author of *Who Stole Feminism?*, witnessed the credibility of this at the 1998 National Coalition for Sex Equity in Education Conference (NCSEE, pronounced 'Nice-ee'):

> A gender-equity instructor from New York University, Dr. Sudan Levin Schlechter, addressed the call-out gap, [calling out answers instead of raising your hand to be recognized], the "problem" of boys getting more teacher attention than girls. She suggested that teachers "create a community of learners" by calling on students alternately: "boy-girl, boy-girl." A vigilant diversity officer from the Aurora public schools in Colorado chastised her: she should have put it "girl-boy, girl-boy."[41]

Another commonly used inclusive pronoun is *their*. Traditionally a plural pronoun with possessive qualities, *their* is sometimes substituted in place of *he/she*. Much to the chagrin of Madame Grammar, the plurality of 'their' has come to also indicate the possessive quality for the singular 'he' and the singular 'she' simultaneously. Whereas other languages retain gender conscious words along with the usage of the masculine form when indicating both men and women, the American English language is losing them.

Let us examine the Spanish language which has engendered words. Typically, the masculine form is indicated by the suffix –o as in amigo (male friend), novio (boyfriend), muchos muchachos (many guys), and doctor or profesor (male doctor and teacher).[xvi] The feminine form is typically signaled with the suffix –a or the absence of suffix –o as in amiga (female friend), novia (girlfriend), muchas muchachas (many girls), and doctora or profesora (female doctor and teacher). If I were relating my experience of having made new friends at a Hoosier Boys State I would say, "Yo tengo los muchos amigos nuevos." If I were to say that I have many friends (guys and gals) at school I would still use the masculine form: *Yo tengo los **muchos amigos** a esculea.* The concept of the dominant masculine form also applies to unconditioned gender roles. When referred together, father (padre) and mother (madre) become los padres (the parents). This morphologic phenomenon holds true for Italian, French, Portuguese, Brazilian Portuguese, German, Serbian, Polish, Russian, and several other languages.

One of the few cases in which politics and contemporary society have left unchallenged the dominance of the specific masculine form is in the word alumni which describes both men (alumni) and women (alumnae) graduates together. Perhaps the craziest and most relevant extreme morphemic proposal to our lexicon is the word *womyn.* Apparently feminists are serious about this independence thing and want no connection to Adam's rib. At least phonetically, *womyn* and *women/woman* sound identical; I suppose that is some consolation...I suppose.

I am aware this ideology of an androgynous vocabulary has not caught on and spread to the general public but remains more confined to the ivory tower. The bad news is that with each course instructed under social androgyny, however, the effects of gender equitists spread. Students' gender

---

[xvi] For the sake of the reader's knowledge, every object in Spanish is proceeded by articles. The articles were omitted for the sake of clarity as my aim was just to show the construction of some words indicate gender. In the above examples the correct phrasing would be un amigo/una amiga and los doctors/las doctoras, for example.

concepts are modified in order to achieve a "new egalitarian order."[xvii] Outside of the ivory tower common, ordinary people may still say stewardess, and congressman, policeman, mailman, and chairman even when their representative or safety official is female. They may use words like lady and gentleman, normal, and history without the slightest notion of being perceived politically incorrect. From this do we gather such people are too lazy or dim to recognize a female policeman is not a man? Of course not. The issue of sexual discrimination most likely never enters the picture to which most feminists might then argue the case that it is all the more reason to stop employing "man" when speaking in general.

The term "mankind" should still be used to refer to both men and women because it is correct. As Jacques Barzun explains, *man* means *human being* both etymologically and by usage ever since the words started at the start of all our languages, which is Sanskrit. "Man does not mean male, except in a special exception which is understood by the context. So it is again ignorance and prejudice that thinks *man* always means *male*. The Bible makes that perfectly clear. I mean, the standard King James Version: 'God created man, male and female.'"[42]

The point I wish to highlight is that academics are stressing a political language movement that would make us conscious of engendered terms. Being that they are in the educational system, we assume teachers are concerned with teaching correct grammar, that they are educating. I contend they are not teaching correct English grammar, but are manipulating curriculum with politics or otherwise irrational motives. The effects of misleading academics through sexual politics are revealed in fascinating detail by Christina Sommers in her book *The War Against Boys* (2000). "The promoters of 'gender fairness' have a great deal of power in

---

[xvii] Christina Sommers adds that the reformers who promote their arcane and undemocratic notion of equality in our schools represent no one but themselves. "But they speak with confidence about gender justice, and many American educators have become persuaded that eliminating 'masculine stereotypes' is a prerequisite to fulfilling the promise of a democratic equality"(98).

our schools," claims Mrs. Sommers, "but they are far too reckless with the truth, far too removed from the precincts of common sense, and far too negative about boys to be properly playing any role in the education of our children."[43] Time invested in reading her research would be well invested.

Of manipulation and politics, certain federal programs bear evidence to feminism's indiscriminateness. By all accounts the women's movement has been one of the most effective in the past century—achieving suffrage, common acceptance in the workplace, high military rank, and television and movie portrayals as professionals or independent persons. Today's youth are growing up in a world where females in the roles of boss or construction worker, police chief or convict, doctor or lawyer, subway operator or Secretary of State are no longer an oddity, a discombobulating shocker.

The effects of feminism have been very successful in eroding manhood through elimination of virtually every male bastion. This has been principally via one particular federal program, Title IX. Title IX was amended to the Education bill of 1972. Basically, its purpose is to introduce women to the many areas outside of the home typically and predominately filled by men. Initially the hope was that more young women would enroll in college and graduate with a degree. They would become the doctors, lawyers, senators, and moneymakers their mothers told them to marry. In the meantime, young women were to actively participate in every sport of interest. It is a popular misconception that the law mandated—opps! humyn-dated—that girls be among those counted on the playing fields. After an initial burst of progress following its passage in 1972, Title IX did little to promote gender equity in intercollegiate athletics during the 1980s, said Andrew Zimbalist in an article printed in *The Chronicle of Higher Education.* The truth of the matter is, sports was not part of the deal when it was initially enacted.[xviii]

[xviii] The bill, which is not a section of the Civil Rights law, pertained to educational programs and was supposed to outlaw sexual discrimination, prevent (illegal) action against males due to past discrimination against females, and prohibit gender quotas in educational programs.

The effect this has had on colleges and universities is tremendous but perhaps not easily or seriously recognized. From the impact of the women's movement many schools turned coed in the late 1960's and 1970's. In 1965 there were 236 men's colleges in the nation. Today, only 4 men's colleges in the nation remain. Notice, I said men's colleges as opposed to single sex. There are currently over 12 times as many female colleges in the country as there are men's colleges. But I digress. Soon there were girl varsity sports (or playing opportunities) at secondary schools and incentives like scholarships to encourage girls to pursue college; more attention was being devoted to the female and women issues. As of this writing, women make up about 57% of the undergraduate population. This fact alone speaks volumes to women's progress in this country. It also weakens the popular claims and contentions of deprived opportunities and academic inferiority believing as I do that a suppressed group enjoying a reversal of fortune can no longer legitimately claim suppression or vitimicy in the classroom. Other than in the headlines there is no 'girls crisis.' In light of many things it appears boys are more on the out. Based on her research Mrs. Sommers says the representation of American girls as apprehensive and academically diminished is not true to the facts. " Girls, allegedly so timorous and lacking in confidence, now outnumber boys in student governments, in honor societies, on school newspapers, and even in debating clubs. Only in sports are the boys still ahead, and women's groups are targeting the sports gap with a vengeance."

According to a recent report issued by the N.C.A.A., women make up approximately 40 percent of Division I athletic scholarship recipients and intercollegiate teams. Citing from the *New York Times'* article written by Lena Williams (November 1999), the head of the N.C.A.A.'s women's athletic committee, Cheryl Levick, is not pleased with 40 percent. (Among all female athletes, 95% of the gains—the most athletic scholarships, competitive atmosphere, and extensive recruiting—are at the Division I level.[44]) Levick is cited as remarking that fairness would only be achieved when women reached the 50 percent mark in participation, scholarships, recruitment, and salaries. Allow me to present the opening three paragraphs.

> Two years ago, the National Collegiate Athletic Association predicted that it would take 10 to 12 years to achieve equality in men's and women's athletic programs at its member schools.
>
> Although there are still inequalities, according to a report issued yesterday by the N.C.A.A., more women are participating in intercollegiate athletics and more women are receiving athletic scholarships, with parity projected in six years:
>
> Since the association issued its last report on disparities between the sexes in 1997, the number of women participating in athletics in Division I has increased by an average of 28 a school. By comparison, the number of male athletes increased by an average of 15 a school.[45]

From the rate of things it would hardly suffice if women reached the fifty percent mark. What then? More importantly, what does 50/50 participation in sports prove other than girls and boys like recreation alike? Is something contributed to society? Perhaps. Ancient Greece, for one, believed the Marathonian stalwart fitness of body and soul was powerful. But to return to the original point, fairness would hardly be gained sufficiently from 50/50 as one can well imagine the immediate implementation of speech codes, sensitivity training[xix], aggression management seminars, and self-esteem workshops along with a more strict criteria of sexual harassment. This interference in athletics by social

---

[xix] For a perspective on the credible effects of sensitization see, for example, Christina Sommers, *The War Against Boys: How Misguided Feminism is Harming Our Young Men.* "Besides wasting precious classroom time, what effect do these "sensitivity" exercises have on the students? Girls cannot fail to be provoked to anger against the male sex, which, they are told, 'learns violent behavior with manhood.' Boys, on the other hand, must feel branded as the violent, callous sex. Can these effects be what the authors of the guide want to achieve"(57)?

reformers is not bemusing at all when you consider they are equal parts Rousseauian romantics, gender-equitists, and socialists. Only in sports are the boys still ahead and zealous women's groups narrow-mindedly work to rewrite that fact. A fellow student once tried to convince me that everything not non-violent was essentially bad, including contact sports. Martyrs of non-violence like Mahatma Ghandi and Dr. Martin King are appropriately esteemed, but the student, like so many others, would do well to recognize conflict, including wars, sometimes begets the security and protection of many lands and people including America.

Cedric Dempsey, president of the National Collegiate Athletic Association, declared, as so many groups do, the endless road of progress still to be traveled. Insisting improvements were slow he said that we must continue to add programs for women and dedicate more resources to women's programs on our campuses at a faster rate. Under the biased interpretations of Cheryl Levick, Cedric Dempsey, and many others, Title IX has taken on a course for the worse (and has been for the past few years). As the numbers show, instead of working toward parity by creating programs for co-eds the new Title IX works to equate opportunities by eliminating men's programs. What is being enforced is a gender-quota system which bluntly does not consider actual athlete interests for either gender. Is it that something for men hinders equality whereas something specifically for women does not? More and more venues, principally men's sports, are being sacrificed in the stated effort of parity. If this is not a clear drive against young men and their preference of pursuits, then how much more convincing is needed? Perhaps a lot if the person believes young men are not being shafted in the first place.

Title IX supporters do not believe the larger picture shows significant net losses for male athletes. Mr. Zimbalist wrote, "I am heartened (Why?) that Cedric Dempsey has issued public declarations that the progress of Title IX is too slow." He concludes, "Until we support women's college sports at similar levels to those of the men—and for as long as a generation—we won't be able to assess their long-run potential." In the meantime, people who are concerned by the modest shrinking of men's sports, advised Zimbalist, should think less about taking resources away from female athletes and more about resources that are wasted at all levels of college athletics. The sluggishness of enforcement is, to say the least, moot and at most only apparent to some people.

Why, sir, should we support one type of sport as we do another? (To assess their long-run potential.) Then what do we do when we come to the fork in assessment? (We assess.) And afterwards do we repeal or cease the program if the tree bore no fruit or do we maintain it out of tradition or optimism that eventually it will prove its worth? The clear effect with established reforms is the difficulty in reforming them once they have been implemented for many years. Reforms, we may as well acknowledge, hitch-hike along that endless road of progress with nothing short of a utopian destination in sight. One camp believes their rights are protected by Title IX while another camp believes its "protection" or the means thereof are unjust.

Do not misunderstand me. The friction is not that boys need more opportunities but that the existing ones need to stop disappearing. Some, though, contend that it is unrealistic to expand women's sports while not bothering men's sports. The author is not arguing for the abolishment of Title IX. Who is proposing taking any resources away from women? The ominous "them" is given in reply. Neither in *The Chronicle of Higher Education* nor my research is anyone cited as wanting to decrease resources for female athletes.

Earlier I mentioned the aim of a government intervention such as Title IX was to increase the representation of an underrepresented group. What happens when that group becomes the majority or ceases to be underrepresented? Do we transfer the cause to the new minority or maintain it for the original recipients though they no longer qualify for it services?

The fact is boys are going colleges in fewer numbers. Nearly 60 percent of all bachelors degrees were earned by women in 1999. According to the U.S. Department of Education, women will outnumber men in higher education programs by 9.2 million to 6.9 million by 2008. Judging by the current pace, Tom Mortenson, a higher education policy analyst says "the graduation line in the year 2068 will be all females."[46] About 1979 women became the majority on campuses of all types (two-year and four-year, public and private, and large and small) and have since narrowed or reversed the gender gap in degree earnings and some areas of studies particularly the humanities.

In light of the gender flip-flop the progress report for Title IX receives high marks for advancing gender equity in post secondary education. In US News and World Report, Brendan I. Koerner reports ("Where the Boys Aren't") on the new gender gap that shows boys opting for the workforce and computer revolution while girls decide to pursue higher education. "The growing split in post-secondary paths might do more to foster gender equality than any constitutional amendment or court decision," says Koerner. "With an edge in education, women could close the salary gap and increasingly move into positions of power—as heads of corporations, presidents of universities, and political leaders."

With gender equity evolving so rapidly why do some reformers dogmatically contend more interference of the law is needed? Do they assume that anything lawful is also legitimate? So what gives? One explanation, it seems to me, is the childish attitude of wanting what another has for the sole sake of wanting, and if that is not achieved, then removing it so no one can have it. This is characteristic of "disillusioned socialists."[xx]

The pattern shows boys more inclined than girls toward athletics and receiving more funds in the way of coaches' salaries, equipment, scholarship, and publicity. Some pounce on this, arguing sexual

---

[xx] F. A. Hayek, *Law, Legislation, and Libert*, vol. 1, 58: If I am not mistaken, this fashionable contempt for 'ideology' or for all general principles or 'isms', is a characteristic attitude of disillusioned socialists who, because they have been forced by the inherent contradictions of their own ideology to discard it, have concluded that all ideologies must be erroneous and that in order to be rational one must do without one.

discrimination and so seek to manipulate Title IX to also encompass sports. For fear of missing the forest for the trees, is the odyssey of college to study and earn a degree—to which women are doing in overshadowing numbers—and make a successful living thereafter or to play sports? If the latter is not the paramount case, then why bother with men's sports? Another explanation for meddling with court orders or constitutional amendments has to do with the impossibility of pleasing everyone all of the time. As printed in "Where the Boys Aren't" listen to what some have to say about the gender-gap:

> Barbara Miller, anthropologist: Every sort of job that's associated with females is also associated with declining status. They're less economically promising in terms of lifetime earnings.
>
> Joan Mudge, director of college counseling at Garrison Forest School (an all-girls college): They [admissions directors] don't come right out and say they're discriminating against our girls, but they are...[claiming] 'Our female applicant pool was just incredible this year.'
>
> Judith Sturnick, director of American Council on Education's Office of Women in Higher Education: We still find that women are more likely to be concentrated in female fields, which have lower pay, fewer opportunities for advancement, and less prestige. Will we set up a separate track for education which will primarily benefit men, which will allow them to enter the job market with higher pay at a higher salary while women continue on the baccalaureate track, end up debt laden, and then wind up three or four years behind in a profession?[47]

I know not whether these women call themselves feminists but they are fault-finders and as Henry David Thoreau said, "Even the fault-finder finds fault in paradise." Never taken into consideration is happiness. Nor is free will considered. Is it too hard to accept that coeds might find

English or psychology more appealing and pleasurable to study than, say engineering or computer science? Are we to forcibly redirect collegians' academic pursuits because of a redistribution of interests: on average, girls like this more so than boys, blacks more so than whites and Asians more so than Americans? Inventing a legislation to "correct" a generalizable redistribution of interests is a ridiculous breach of justice, a corrupt use of law. Collegians are capable of using their God-given free will to will their own improvement.

Socialists need to stop looking at persons as nothing other than raw material to be molded in equal proportions collectively. Academic feminism appears to me at odds with the amazing success of coeducation because of the lack of remonstrance of young men who are more and more going for the big paychecks, computer jobs, and technical schools after high school. Some people don't like this. The griping seems ironic to many people, especially those who remember when most colleges were all male. Then again, maybe irony does not enter the picture if, after all, coeducation is what was really desired and now that all but 25 coed schools are mostly women the co-in coeducation is quickly disappearing. But what progressive cause is responsible for this? I will leave you to ponder that.

Ms.'s Mudge, Sturnick, and others who share the sentiment of coeds' concentration in particular fields mistake materialism and status and recognition with success ("lower pay, fewer opportunities for advancement, and less prestige"). They devote little consideration to the students' academic achievement, happiness, and ambition for a family. "Do not confuse having a career with having a life," said Hillary Clinton. "They are not the same."

If, indeed, gender equality is evolving from the split in one sex's decision to enter the workplace and the other the campus why are some folks calling on constitutional amendments to intervene? They are soliciting the law because higher education ain't what it use to be. This has some worried that women's preferred studies reinforce their secondary position in the economy. "When there begins to be a predominance of female members in any area, the value of that area goes down," said Judith Sturnick. To a lot of people, including feminists, it looks like the increasing feminization could lead to a general devaluation of post-secondary education. Ms. Sturnick even asks whether it is possible that we are devaluing higher education. The backlash to feminism seems to be the notion that if girls can do it, then it must not be worthwhile. If degrees are judged fruitless, then where is our education system headed? And if the direction of our system looks unfavorable then what does that mean for the nation's future? This concern coupled with the typical pressure from male peers to minimize intellectual enthusiasm is also contributory to boys' college ambitions.

Margaret Miller, president of the American Association for Higher Education (AAHE) agrees, saying "Being good in school is associated with femininity."[48] So long as education remains a societal priority then education will remain a barometer of sorts for success. In the *US News* article the author writes:

> If college degrees remain an entrée to wealth and status in the 21st Century, males may have to get used to the same second-class status that American women so long endured, as highly educated females become the majority among the nations' intellectual, economic, and even power elite.

Early into the feature Mr. Koerner advanced "that's assuming higher education remains the key to upward mobility—a big "if," warn some who foresee a time not too distant when degrees are not so prized, and skipping college might just be a wise career choice." Reports show that Title IX is a success. Therefore should it a) cease activity or b) expand to include the endangered male collegian? If the minority cease being the minority, then they no longer qualify for services on behalf of minorities anymore than a poor man turned rich can still claim welfare benefits. But wait, caution feminist academics, boys still dominate in sports participation. Regarding Title IX's function could this explain why the new model is stepping from it proper bounds and into **extra** curriculum?

While the amendment exists to affect equality between the sexes in general, the new Title IX first and foremost targets education through athletics. Under the Clinton Administration Norma Cantu of the Department of Education is effectively obliterating male athletics with her vehicle of *proportionality*. Under her three criteria for a school to dodge discrimination charges boys simply can not win. So "eager to avoid charges of discrimination that trigger the punitive provisions of Title IX, many schools and school districts have hired trained 'equity' coordinators."[49] In a state of PC ridiculousness and anxiety "no school today can afford to take the risk of being charged with tolerating behavior [however minute, innocuous, or mistaken] that offends a female student."

To begin, the college might try eliminating enough male athletes to make the percentage of female athletes match the percentage of actual female enrollment to avoid discrimination charges. In other words, accomplish proportionality. Secondly, the college could demonstrate or show a history of continuous increase in female participation. The third way for a university to operate unscathed is to prove that it has accommodated every co-ed's interest. Is this agenda one sided? Is proportionality combating discrimination or is it a bureaucratically, disguised version of discrimination with no end in sight? I, for one, do not believe there is such a thing as reverse discrimination. The very idea is the sophism of white man's burden. What are the consequences of proportionality—including long term—on education?

Cantu's proportionality test is invalid and unreliable because it only sees things as male versus female. There are many other demographics that operate in choosing higher education and extracurricular activities to boot. Kimberly Schuld, of the Independent Women's Forum, is at odds with the proportionality test. She argues it "does not take into account the higher number of older, returning, working, parenting students on campus who may not have the interest, ability, time or energy to participate in varsity sports."ˣˣⁱ Like many rational minds on this topic, Ms. Schuld thinks "proportionality" should be done away with. The Independent Women's Forum is a nationwide organization whose three principles of individual liberty, personal responsibility, and equal opportunity for all Americans are "offended" by the current application of Title IX.[50] Why? Probably because gender-equity rules are more slanted than they are equal.

Since it is part of a federal program, only the President of the United States can quash the proportionality rule. Similar to the positions of a Supreme Court Justice, the U.S. Vice President or a tenured professor, Norma Cantu has job security to be envied—only the President **can** remove her. President Clinton is not going to remove her but maybe President-select George W. will. Whether or not Norma Cantu remains in office, clearly the proportionality test should be reformed in some fashion, preferably dissolution. Perhaps it could be amended to count only full time students, 18-24 year olds with experience or intense interest in sports, as Kimberly Schuld suggested. This demographic, when you think about it, is the real qualified applicant pool.

Dale Anderson, a concerned individual, is leading a petition drive asking for the next President (and courts/authorities) to overturn or reinterpret the proportionality rule. Citing Anderson from a nearly full page advertisement in the Wrestling USA Magazine (September 15, 1999):

> The first way [to evade charges of discrimination] is clearly a quota that only eliminates males. The second and third ways of complying with title IX always and only increase female participation. Presently 4-5 males are being dropped under the proportionality rule for every female added. At the present rate wrestling and all other Olympic sports opportunities will soon be gone.[51]

---

xxi Title IX pushers would do well to know that for undergraduate students 30% are over the age of 30 with the average age being 28 years; single parents account for 11%; and a big roughly 80% of undergraduate students clock in 15 hours of work in addition to school.

Neitzsche commented on the decline of Ancient athletics. He wrote that whenever an occasion arose to enumerate the demagogues of the day, the adherents of the "good old times" would mention both names in the same breath. To the influence of Socrates and Euripides, continued Neitzsche, they attributed the fact that the old Marathonian stalwart fitness of body and soul was being sacrificed more and more to a dubious enlightenment that involved the progressive degeneration of the powers of body and soul.[52] I think Mr. Anderson might agree. He has grounds to be concerned about the future of scientific wrestling. Wrestling will be a recurring theme throughout this section.

Of all the Olympic sports, it has suffered the most casualties without pause or fail. Wrestling is being hit the hardest because it has the least draw of female participation and not as much pull as football or basketball. It is unmistakably a men's sport. It is also traditional, stemming farther back than ancient Rome. As expected of extreme feminism any legacy of maleness is something to be abolished. However, there are some female wrestlers. There is even the U.S. Girls Wrestling Association (USGWA). Therefore the retronism male wrestling is really not an oxymoron. Regardless, collegiate wrestling is steadily becoming extinct for no other convincing ground other than more boys than girls go out for it. Plain and simple, college wrestling is being swept under the mat because girls, on average, are not drawn to participate. Doubtless, there will ever be a reversal in gender appeal to the activity. Looming is the concern, "What does the future hold for wrestling programs?"

Before going on with the natural and societal upheld explanations for girls' disinclination to wrestling, let us examine an overview of Cantu's damage. Despite the target of male wrestling, Mr. Zimbalist does not acknowledge the gravity of the situation. In *The Chronicle* he writes, "...the number of colleges and universities sponsoring male wrestling teams fell only from 264 in 1993-94 to 246 in 1997-98, a modest decline of 6.8 percent." Between 1993 and 1999 roughly 43 colleges and universities of all divisions closed their wrestling programs.[53] With the data of one additional year the sum of dropped wrestling programs more than doubled. In the span of one year more wrestling teams lost sponsorship than the whole "modest decline" between 1993 to 1998. In general, all male athletics are falling rapidly. Most recently, Greg Louganis' alma mater, the University of Miami has decided to drop its men's swimming/diving and crew programs to 'avoid' the punishment of Title IX gender-equity rules. Making this situation all the more startling is the fact the university fashioned over a dozen Olympic divers.

The 1997 data from the NCAA's five-year Gender Equity Report showed that 20,000 male athletes no longer existed.[54] The big pay-off?— an increase in female athletes by 5,800. According to this, for every female added, four males were withdrawn. Another unbelievable fact showed that between 1992 and 1997 Division III institutions added 178 female athletic opportunities and cut varsity opportunities for men by more than 9,000. Whoa, for every female added 20 males were dumped. Mr. Zimbalist reported the last three years saw a six percent growth of male athletes and "from 1978 to 1996 the number of men's teams in all three NCAA divisions, in fact, increased by 74."

Yet, for all of the numbers, the General Accounting Office's 1999 report does not produce data supportive of the need for more resources to satisfy the 'tremendous' female athletic drive. (The preceding statistics were located at **www.wrestlingusa.com/titlenine.html**.) In order to stave off the dogmatic gender-quota we likely end up with as Kimberly Schuld put it, "rich schools creating varsity sports out of hobbies, and the cash-strapped schools cutting back on men's positions to match existing women's positions." (Is the University of Miami strapped for cash or strapped for cash **and** fearful of proportionality?)

Now that we have given considerable attention to Title IX and its effects let us return to the issue of gender differences over wrestling. One of the first forms of games we see children—boys and girls—engage in is rough and tumble play where there is no intent of harm. Toddlers, we can observe, like to roll around and jump on each other; playfully wrestling just like cubs and puppies and kittens. Prior to puberty the physical differences are relatively inconsequential. Before getting too comfortable and crying bloody murder to society for separating boys and girls it is worth knowing that aggression is more of a masculine trait than a female one. Thus even minus the intent of malice and injury, boys are three times more likely than girls to indulge in rough and tumble play.[xxii]

Sadly, our little boys' exuberance are increasingly being railroaded as attention-deficit disorder (ADD) which, in turn, is addressed—suppressed—with Ritalin. What goes through the minds of the primary decision-makers? (No, let's not take the time to play with him and redirect his energies. Instead, let's accept the diagnosis and have a "special" child who is excused from gym class, allergic to outdoors, and can't socialize with his mates.) Boys' energies and lack of focus are too easily dubbed behavioral or developmental disorders, resulting in a disproportionate number of them winding up in special education or detention wards. "By zapping them of their 'Zeus Juice'," argues one Wabash student, "Ritalin has made its victims into the docile 'perfect little gentlemen'—i.e., girls with penises—overbearing mothers always have desired."[55] The feature in US News touched on the topic of favoritism which some believe elementary and secondary teachers foster. They argue that the tendency of boys to be rambunctious, to ignore directions, and to produce sloppy assignments, writes Mr. Koerner, draws the ire of teachers who prefer more well-behaved, manageable girls.[56]

What is more, as early as 3.5 years old, children might began to be sociodramatic, a (social)psychological term inferring they pick gender specifics. Thus, before adolescence, children adopt gender roles; shop for gender role schemas. Observe a nursery school or kindergarten and you will see a distinction between boys and girls as they identify with the same gender. Boys tend to be in large groups, physically aggressive and exaggerative in talk. In contrast, girls stick to small, intimate

---

[xxii] Class notes. Professor Stephanie Delpaine-Gadient, Fall semester, 1999.

groups. They exhibit greater, more frequent communication. As we grow older, biological and social transformations coincide to further distinguish the genders.

Our once almost identical body shape turns distinct in adolescence (Malina, 1990).[57] Primary sex characteristics like menarche and fertility, and secondary sex characteristics such as outer body development indicate sexual maturation. With the menstrual cycle comes a signal for the girl to learn to adapt to the new pattern—cycle—of her body. What if the calmness of the cycle routinely 'acts up' around the winter months when school wrestling is conducted or during spring when international wrestling (e.g., freestyle and Greco-Roman) is in effect, what then? This is not the case for the male body. Menstruation brings on occasional cramping and some episodes can be painful enough to preclude regular activities (the delicacy of this issue perhaps is addressed by the USGWA). This variable and others do not lend themselves to competitive wrestling especially the issue of weight gain in a realm where weight loss is the thing.

These changes signal approaching womanhood and fertility. Cut it anyway you like, young men and women grappling just does not look cool or socially appropriate.

Regarding secondary sex characteristics, our new physical attributes as if to have eaten of the Tree of Knowledge cause us to pay more attention to our body image and those of potential lovers and mates in a new light. Men typically get taller, noticeably stronger, and wider in the shoulders. Women typically get rounder and wider in the hips. (The hips are the center of gravity. Wrestlers want to control their opponents' center of gravity and disrupt his balance. Bigger hips produce a bigger and easier target.)

If a first grader can be accused of sexual harassment for pecking a classmate on the cheek[xxiii], if a joke—crude or not—constitutes grounds

---

[xxiii] A few years back in North Carolina, a six-year-old boy received a day's suspension for pecking a classmate on her cheek. The U.S. Department of Education (Office of Civil Rights) informed the country that the little Casanova's kiss did not constitute sexual harassment. Heterophobia is alive.

for a multi-million dollar lawsuit, if sexual harassment can be levied because she doesn't *recall* consenting to sex, then what on earth must we make of aggressive full body grappling between the sexes?[xxiv] Since no wrestler wants to be pinned then would that not mean that he beat her against her wishes? That he *forced* himself on her? Can you say the "R" word? Millions of hungry lawyers and bitter feminists—the makeup of what Patai dubs the Sexual Harassment Industry (SHI)[xxv]—can and frequently do. According to Patai, the SHI has become a social reform movement so enthused with hatred that it will probably not remain "sound and whole" for very long.[58]

Not to belabor the evident gender differences but in the face of 'proportionality's' efficacy the topic begs sound argumentation.

Men have greater doses of testosterone than women. This hormone which has recently come under attack for inducing everything from male insensitivity and misogyny to a new! disorder called Adonis complex causes rapid arousal and rapid shifts of emotions. Excitement and exuberance might come from small stimuli while more intense stimulation will likely manifest violence and aggression (e.g., fights, rodeo, use of weaponry, drag racing, contact sports). Masculine toughness

---

[xxiv] Supreme Court Justice Anthony Kennedy warned in his dissenting opinion (*Davis case*) against the Court's recent ruling (5—4) in favor of applying sexual harassment laws to schoolchildren "[The majority's decision] will breed a climate of fear that encourages school administrators to label even the most innocuous of child conduct sexual harassment"(as quoted in Sommers, 2000, 69). Other Justices who voted in the minority were Antonin Scalia, William Rehnquist, and Clarence Thomas. The author of *The War Against Boys* concurs, "Schools, fearful of ruinous lawsuits, will treat normal boys as protoharassers"(71).

[xxv] Patai refers to contemporary feminists and their preoccupation with sexual behavior and male dominance as the Sexual Harassment Industry. They look to sue men and corporations. She says: "What started, arguably, as a utopian impulse to improve women's lot has, it is now clear, come to entangle not only men but also women, and not only heterosexuals but also homosexuals, in the quixotic pursuit of a sanitized environment in which the beast of male sexuality will at long last have been vanquished"(11).

is still an accepted cultural concept amidst all the rhetoric that it is a relic of the Neanderthal, the undeveloped man. No thank you ladies, keep your white feathers for some other chap.

For whatever reasons, intercollegiate wrestling just does not appeal to girls enough for them to compete aggressively. Needless to say, it is a different story for boys. Norma Cantu along with bureaucrats and federal judges, are mistaken in trying to malign masculine nature and eliminate appropriate outlets like competitive athletics. Athletic directors are forced to eliminate the number of male sports with revenue less than football and basketball in order to satisfy the gender equity issue. Title IX was not written to be used this way. To quote Schuld, "it not only ignores legitimate differences between men and women, but legitimate differences among women. We are not all athletes, and we are not all scholars."[59] Men's sports are being killed off. The proverbial Wild Man is being hunted down.[xxvi] Male exuberance is being demonized instead of channeled into productive outlets. This trend is bound to suffer repercussions. To impugn his desire to become "one of the boys," says Mrs. Sommers, is to deny that a boy's biology determines much of what he prefers and is attracted to. In her opinion (and mine), when education theorists deny boys' nature, they are in a position to cause them much misery.[60]

The authors of a child development textbook sum up the conclusions of two researchers (James Harrison, 1984; and Miriam Miedzian, 1991) that support this point.

> A society that turns positive masculine tendencies such as courage, independence, and competitiveness (all of which might have an evolutionary biological base) into such negative male traits as recklessness, callousness, and 'an egocentric and often obsessive need to be dominant and to win' is bound to suffer violent consequences.[61]

[xxvi] In *Iron John: A Book About Men* (1990), author and poet Robert Bly expounds on the virtues of the Wild Man—"the hairy man"—who protects and mentors a young boy through manhood and maturity.

In response to the traditional patriarchy that had long been the way of America, the women's movement sought to leave that trend with their fathers. Rather than have a 1950's breadwinner man, women suddenly wanted their beau to get in touch with his feminine side before getting acquainted with theirs. Men were to be tender, capable and willing to cry in public—friends. Around the late 1960s and early 1970s clothes and hairstyles lost gender specific qualities for the most part. Boys and girls, both, wore gear like hip-huggers, bell-bottoms, platforms, and to a great extent long hair or Afros or permanents. Clothes were unisex (long before Calvin Klein). So what, big deal, right? All futuristic movies have us sporting identical metallic uniforms anyway. Many areas of the workforce also saw a shift in employees. According to Vance Packard's book, *The Sexual Wilderness,* females made up two-thirds of the increase in the US workforce between 1947 to 1962.

The deeper thorn—the real problem—was the psychological alteration that occurred. Male heroes or ladies' men[xxvii] got the boot. Stepping up to plate were yoga instructors, exercise gurus, folk musicians/poets (that lucky bunch win either way), and basic emotional therapists, tree-huggers, draft-dodgers, male feminists. Robert Bly, author of *Iron John: A Book About Men,* has done a great deal of research on the contemporary man and contemporary man's present confusion about masculinity. Bly wrote:

> During the sixties, another sort of man appeared. The waste and violence of the Vietnam war made men question whether they knew what an adult male really was...Meanwhile, the feminist movement encouraged men to actually look at women, forcing them to become conscious of concerns and sufferings that the Fifties male labored to avoid. As men began to examine women's history and women's sensibility, some men began to notice what

---

[xxvii] E.g., Joe Dimaggio, John Wayne, George Washington, Frank Sinatra, James Bond, Franklin Roosevelt, Hercules, Sir Winston Churchill, Arthur Ashe, Iron John, Bruce Lee, Theodore Roosevelt, soldiers.

was called their *feminine* side and pay attention to it. This process continues to this day, and I would say that most contemporary men are involved in it in some way.[62]

The mission: more *gentle* and less **man**. A popular bumper sticker and poster of the times read, "WOMEN SAY YES TO MEN WHO SAY NO."[xxviii] Yet, as Patai wisely points out, this patience is no sound safeguard "since any woman can change her mind *after* she has made the first move."[63]

The purpose was noble. Why should one endure needless stress and ulcers all because he suppressed his emotions to a dangerous degree? Cry man, your dad just passed away. Go ahead and hug your son, he just graduated. Kiss him. Embrace him. There is nothing wrong or unmanly about this—this much the women's cause was right in stressing. But they took it too far. They failed to realize that men do grieve and that they always have, just out of the sight of females. Men let down their guard of stoicism, collective-ness, and machismo in the company of other men. It is true that men don't share their feelings like women do. This seems to be a constant. Just as they did as schoolgirls, women tend to congregate in smaller, intimate groups, sharing greater verbal communication. In contrast, men bond with their peers simply by being in their company; maybe drinks and grunts are part of the mix, maybe there is not much talk exchanged, maybe there is not much anything comparable to what women do; but what does that mean?

Feminists want the feminized or *soft* male. While it was soliciting the less pronounced feminine traits of man, the feminist movement, unfortunately was directly discouraging masculinity at the same time. As a result, America got a crop of "secure" young men who would not (and possibly could not)

---

xxviii I first came across this hippie ideal in Bly's book, *Iron John*. On the surface, the message was anti-war propaganda, implying that draft-dodgers and Vietnam protesters were real men for refusing not to fight. These women preferred men of white feathers. The latent, sexual message was telling men to wait for the woman to make the first move.

make a decision without their better half, men who proudly shied away from athletics, participated, albeit silently, in women's groups and classes, who left disciplining up to the mother, who wanted to 'just be friends and talk' like bosom buddies. Woman was liberated, by God, and she wanted gents liberated enough who would lend the match to help burn her bras. (On second thought, perhaps I too hastily judge that last gesture.)

The antidote was trying to correct a supposed problem. The supposed problem was man's seemingly inherent tendencies for aggression or control. I could pour out a list of empirical studies that show this to be the case, but our eyes will do just fine. Look around. Think back. Males play rougher, act tougher, engage in more physical conflicts, are more competitive, command military strategies, tend to bait risk and trouble, inhabit gymnasiums and weight-rooms, lead nations, organizations, businesses, seek public office. On average, American men are taller/bigger and stronger than American women. Big and strong are advantageous characteristics for stability and survival. The English suffix morpheme *-er* on words like bigger and stronger denote a comparative quality, meaning "more." Thus, some people have or are more of something while other people have or are less of the same. As a result, there exists a distinction, a separation of sorts. But Openness, with its collective mentality opposes any difference, individuality, dissimilarity.

Champions of Openness do not invest much stock in biology or any science save political science. [Sexual]Politics is the thing; hence our present bother with political correctness. Everything—religion, formal schooling, recreation, clothing, metabolism, physical urges, employment—is reanalyzed and discovered to be an oppressive social construct constructed by white men[xxix]. The Openness movement is not founded on nature. What is this word inherent, they ask? What is meant by innate, they challenge?

[xxix] "An article in *HealthGate* (May 31, 2000) examined why men compete. The PC police woult tell you men and women have the same competitive drives—they're just raised differently. Anthropologists say otherwise. The most aggressive males impregnated

An excerpt of Marilyn Frye's works *Willful Virgins: Essays in Feminism* (1976-1992) trumpets:

> Female heterosexuality is not a biological drive or an individual woman's erotic attraction or attachment to another human animal which happens to be male. Female heterosexuality is a set of social institutions and practices defined and regulated by patriarchal kinship system, by both civil and religious law, and by strenuously enforced mores and deeply entrenched values and taboos. Those definitions, regulations, values and taboos are about male fraternity and the oppression and exploitation of women. They are not about love, human warmth, solace, fun, pleasure, or deep knowledge between people.[64]

All the cosmetics in the world could not help these biology anarchists save face for their blunderous praise of Dr. John Money's now infamous John/Joan case. After a circumcision mishap on the 8-month old child, Dr. Money advised the parents to raise the boy as a girl. The waterloo for Money's research and feminists' arguments that sexual identity results from learned gender roles or cultural socialization came when Joan, fully oblivious to the dark family secret, began rejecting femaleness as a teenager. Joan went back to his innate—i.e., natural, God-given—male identity. All the Barbies and pink hues neither superceded biology nor altered John's sexual orientation!

Through surgery, John's 'man power' has been returned (though he cannot procreate) and today he is a happily married family man. The John/Joan case will forever loom over anti-biology theorists. Despite this, I am not surprised that heavy Feminist rhetoric still regards sexual

---

the most females, so aggressiveness became a desirable genetic trait. Genes direct aggressiveness in males through testosterone, which tends to be higher in aggressive people and those put in competitive situations. But social scientists caution that runaway testosterone isn't necessarily good for relationships and interactions between people," according to recent issue of *Muscular Development*.

overtures—increasingly tagged sexual harassment—as "patriarchal power" rather than biology or natural sexual attraction.[65] Without this mating process of courtship how are we to get each other's attention with the hope of bonding? Arranged marriages? If we continue to make mountains out of molehills sexual advances and unauthorized (that word sounds so out of place!) flirting will become legislated crimes.

Do not misunderstand me. The existence and seriousness of repeated unwarranted offences is not being mitigated. Such behavior is clearly in violation of liberty, property, and comfort. Transgressions of this degree clearly legitimately constitute harassment. At this juncture law should enter the picture because its proper function is to keep us from harming others. Law is force and it is defensive.

By the same token I cannot condone overreaction whereby an "offensive" remark is quickly spun into sexual harassment. I fear two things will come to pass from this unhealthy tension. The first is that women's accusations of sexual harassment will increasingly be prejudged "crying wolf," arousing as much concern as an activated car alarm. The other concern is that sexual reformers will have involved law to the point where discourse and intercourse are authoritatively scheduled and regulated. You may call it Orwellian or even crazy but do not call it impossible and far-fetched. Bottom line: biology matters. Men and women are different and that is why civilization depends on the duality of the sexes.

In critiquing John Rawls' *A Theory of Justice* (1970), Allan Bloom summarizes Rawls to mean, "discriminateness is a moral imperative because its opposite is discrimination."[66] Many advocates of the Openness philosophy take issue with men and women general dissimilarities to each other. Men's attributes of size, strength, and phallus are demonized, seen as oppressive weapons that maintain societal constructs of men and masculinity and women and femininity. More bizarre, the 1970s' male was convinced that he was bad and uncontrollably dangerous to women and himself. Not wanting to be bad, he tried to forget his masculine tendencies; suppress virtually any scintilla of machismo. America's new man wanted—nay! exercised—his feminine side.

Introducing the soft male who delighted in poetry and philosophy, who avoided haircuts, who got in touch with his inner child, felt the female in himself, who regretted his innate contribution to the evil patriarchy, who wanted to be just human (as opposed to man), who hung out with women, wanted to be protected and cared for, who not only suppressed pride in his penis but, also, expressed disgust for being cursed with one—the man who said, "No."

In his first book, *Refusing To Be A Man: Essays on Sex and Justice*, male feminist John Stoltenberg actually believes "nothing is less of an instrument of ecstasy and more of an instrument of oppression than the penis."[67] Oh brother! —or should we say sister? Presumably, the soft male wants to be more like a female. This new man wants to be "free"; that is to say, to have the freedom to cry more, to experience more expressed emotions, tenderness, even. After three decades, I ask, is he free?

Stepping back from the big picture, Robert Bly looks at it from both sides: the poet in him sees the importance and beauty in guys developing their feminine consciousness (he calls them lovely, valuable people) while the man in him senses there is something wrong.[68] "The male in the past twenty years has become more thoughtful, more gentle," said Mr. Bly. "But by this process he has not become more free…You quickly notice the lack of energy in them. They are life-preserving but not exactly life-giving. The strong or life-giving women who graduated from the sixties, so to speak, or who have inherited an older spirit, played an important part in producing this life-preserving, but not life-giving, man."[69] Bly goes on to remark on the union of these softer men and harder women, saying, that, for a time, it seemed like a sound arrangement, "but we've lived with it long enough now to see that it isn't working out."[70]

Openness induces disgust in one's self while supposedly teaching about the virtues of another. Presumably, it is more appropriate to esteem others over one's esteem of self. In enlightening the world to women's issues, men—if they sincerely wanted to understand and commiserate—were made to concede their irreversible role in the whole cosmos of things. In short, to hate self. The published platform and fire of modern feminism can not be commendable as its clear effects on American maleness (and heterosexuality) can be summed in one word: emasculation, or as Daphne Patai would assert, heterophobia. Emasculated males are like human oxen in that they are more passive, less threatening, less powerful, and more easily able to be led. Both are psychologically altered tools. 'Twixt the difference of the two? Whereas the bull has no choice in his physical castration, some men, however, yield and succumb to the rhetoric that emotionally and psychologically castrates them.

Take John Stoltenberg, for example. Mr. Stoltenberg has come to hate self because he hates the idea of being a man. In another of his books, *End of Manhood: A Book for Men of Conscience*, the author recommends his male readers—"penised humans"—trade in maleness (and masculinity) for "selfhood."[71] Or take the underclassman, for example, who regards his gender a mere construct and insists on being just a human. Everything about this student from his physical mannerisms to his ideas and voice inflection reinforce his renouncement of masculinity. And for the lad who thinks his machismo is fading, Mr. Stoltenberg provides a top ten list of ways men can fake masculinity like, say, start a war, or whack off inside someone you're hurting, believe in a butch god, or rape someone.[72]

In the immortal words of Charlie Brown, "Good grief!" Indeed, male sexual passion is maligned as sinful because it culminates in sexism.[73]

With so much focus spent on getting young men to spark acquaintance with their inner woman and inner child why has there been such little counsel for men to approach their inner self, the "deep male"?[74] Is it because the deep male is scarier than the internal woman? Perhaps, but does that mean the deep male is worse? According to the tale interwoven through *Iron John*, the deep male symbolizes the Hairy Man ("a large primitive being covered with [rusty reddish] hair down to his feet"[75]) found at the bottom of the pond, and, later, imprisoned in an iron cage in the courtyard, hence the nickname, Iron John. Today's desensitized, feminized, industrialized, sanitized, and politically correct society discourages modern man's exploration of his dormant "ancient hairy man." Confused and unhappy men like Mr. Stoltenberg and the underclassman are too soft, frightened, and brainwashed to journey down into their psyches to contact this Wild Man. Has anyone in our times confronted the Hairy Man? Mr. Bly thought so. "Freud, Jung, and Wilhelm Reich are three investigators who had the courage to go down into the pond and to accept what they found there. The job of contemporary men is to follow them down."[xxx] This bucketing-out process was something he believed the 80's and 90's male shied away from doing, and it is something I deem the new century male will need much coaching to begin.

As I pause from writing, a scene in Fox network's adult sitcom "Alley McBeal" has three men dancing with an infant in a public restroom to the tune Barry White's "You're My First, My Last, My Everything." The mood is interrupted when a woman walks in and asks what the hell are they doing. One guy actually replies that he [the baby] likes dancing. Having enough of that I channel surf and stop on NBC's legal drama, "Law & Order." A female attorney asks her older male colleague what it was called before "we invented the terms 'date rape' and 'sexual harassment'?" He replies with a smirk, "Boys will be boys." (Subsequent commercials previewed that "Dateline" was doing an expose on an alleged sex offender. The narrator announces something to the effect, "Would you want this educator around your children? Are your children safe at school? Watch 'Dateline' next!")

With Openness blurring gender specifics we have an almost mainstream display of boys wanting to be girls (effemination) and girls wanting to be boys (see Sigmund Freud's theory on penis envy). The

---

[xxx] The author does comment that some modern men have brought the Hairy Man up into the "courtyard", meaning that he is observable to others. "That is some advance over keeping the Hairy Man in a cellar…[nonetheless] in either place, he's still in a cage," 70

phrase 'sexual orientation' is now a household word. It is no longer a given that a boy is referring to girls when talking about dating problems or love interests, and vice versa. The soft male of two decades past ushered in the prevalence and encouraged the confidence of the openly gay man. Since it was intellectual and trendy to be in touch with his feminine side why not just fully embrace it and redeem himself by becoming as Sally Miller Gearhart calls them in her novel, *The Wanderground* (1980), a *gentle*. Simply put, be less of the man in 'gentleman'.

Apparently the notion that man was meant to have relations with woman is an illusion trumped up by the insecurity of the establishment. Deborah Sterns, author of *Gendered Sexuality: The Privileging of Sex and Gender in Sexual Orientation* argues that all sexual orientation is socially constructed.[76] It is no surprise that the soft male ushered in the present saliency of gay pride in the land. Because of unifying the genders; i.e., humans or unisex, the feminist application of Openness is one of the factors that I contend stimulated the current gay revolution. Homosexuality has always been around. History has recorded several notables by name. Some folks (I know not what to call them) are always anxious to out historic and popular figures, illuminating anything remotely close to homoeroticism (by today's standards).

For instance the relationship of Sesame Street's Bert and Ernie became the target of inquiring—more like perverted—minds a few years back. More recently, gay activist Larry Kramer accuses Abraham Lincoln of homosexuality in his yet to be completed book, *The American People*. College is wasted on some people. Yes, homosexuals have been around since before Sodom and Gomorrah yet, the key phrase is "nationwide saliency," meaning that homosexuality is becoming a more tolerable lifestyle in mainstream America.

Looking at the previous decade alone, the 1992 election of Arkansas Governor Bill Clinton to the Oval Office brought the promise of repealing the ban on gays in the military. This campaign promise which was greeted with pink balloons at many of his campaign stops, was eventually reconsidered, compromised, and became, instead, the "Don't ask, don't tell, don't pursue" policy. As it currently stands, neither military recruiters nor anyone else can inquire about anyone's sex life. By the same token, personnel with strong homosexual inclinations can neither openly display nor tell people they are gay. The military is relieved. Gay rights supporters are not. As the French say, "C'est la vie!"

Most of the presidential candidates for the 2000 election indicated their goal to make society more open and responsive to feelings of the gay community. The question of gay rights has been posed at the televised debates. A shocker during Clinton's first run for office was when a young woman asked whether he preferred boxers or briefs. The even bigger surprise was that he actually answered it. We have moved from publicly inquiring of politicians' choice of underwear (and thanks to the explicit Ken Starr Report, the politicians' sexual creativity) to their thoughts on choice of sex partners. What next are we to be opened to?

Many job applications with the mandated exception of the military now inform they do not discriminate against sexual orientation. (In May 2000 San Francisco passed an ordinance prohibiting employers from discriminating against fat people. I imagine modeling agencies will soon be required to sponsor short people, round people, tall people, people of color, old folks, handicapped persons, midgets, and ugly people, too.)

Walt Disney amusement parks have taken to celebrating Gay Day (despite boycotts from the Southern Baptist Convention). Walt Disney Co., which acquired Capital Cities/ABC Inc. in 1995, aired the sitcom "Ellen" whose title character, played by real life lesbian, Ellen Degeneres, came out in an episode three years ago. The show was quickly cancelled. Before Disney came along ABC already had a prominent gay character (also played by a real life homosexual) in the teenage drama "My So Called Life." Also, a much-hyped episode of "Roseanne" where the title character (played by Roseanne Arnold) intimately kisses another woman marked the ABC lineup. Notice a pattern? All the major networks have programs with openly gay characters that are featured frequently or on a semiregular basis. In show business—if it works for one station, then churn and churn out some more.

The Web site Gay, Lesbian, Bisexual Television Characters documented approximately 200 gay characters from 1991 to present.[77]

Cable TV, always more risqué and less censored, is not lost on the formula. MTV, for one, broadcasts a soapy teen soap opera called "Undressed"—i.e., open: *having no protective cover...undo...come into view*—which has every predictable profile and emotional fallout. There is the Black ballplayer trying to escape his thuggish boys from the hood and make it to the pros, the prima donna slut (a.k.a. "liberated woman"), the stud jock, some bickering sisters, the stud pretty boy, computer geek, the stud cousin, the political prude or virgin, the plain old stud, weird video store clerk, more girls with radiant unclogged pores, and, of course, the openly gay couple who argue because the one is unnerved that the other might be still attracted to women, his ex-boyfriend or worse. "All My Children," eat your hearts out.

Cartoons are not left out. "The Simpsons" (Fox) has one episode, in particular, that guest starred camp director John Waters in which Homer, afraid that Water's queerness might rub off on Bart, goes to great lengths to keep Bart from turning gay. One attempt has Homer and his buddies taking Bart to a steel factory so that he could see real men doing tough manly work only to discover that they walked into a gay underground dance pit. Cable's "South Park" (Comedy Central) in addition to its trademark toilet humor and profanity frequently features gay jokes. The cartoon even has a character named Big Gay Al who runs a petting sanctuary for gay animals searching for refuge. The running joke is that Kyle's dog is gay.

Without ambiguity primetime television is pulling gay characters from the closet. In what was once cautioned "a very special episode" Roseanne's lesbian kiss, for example—the occasional gay plot is now a typical fixture. Today, we see gay characters whose lifestyles are only one aspect of who they are, says Mr. Sopko of the *Gary Post Tribune*. Just like real-life folk, we see gay television characters in all sorts of professional positions including law, government ("Spin City") and medicine ("ER" and "Chicago Hope").

And what about other areas?

"Then, there's Jack McPhee, the gay high school football player who is preparing to attend prom with his college boyfriend on "Dawson's Creek." Mr. Sopko continues, "An impeding kiss has many viewers...wondering if the camera will pull away from the act."[xxxi]

The point to be made is that America is experiencing a homosexual revolution. For instance, 1999 marked the first year of the Great Lakes Conference Association's (GLCA) annual GLBT workshop—Gay, Lesbian, Bisexual, Transgender workshop. Liberal intellects convened to discuss and learn about and accept several new sexes. To my chagrin my college participated in the GLBT Conference. Still, how learning about such alternative and counter-productive sex lifestyle benefits the greater good of the campus (or any campus) is beyond me. In tune with the collective GLBT, the college has its own little version of an Openness club called 'shOUT (Wabash Out). The play on words is encouragement for the "questioning and supportive" student-body (and employees) to open up and exit the closets. 'shOUT perfectly illustrates Openness. At best, its objective can be called a stretch as it purports to encompass every preference imaginable:

> 'shOUT is the gay, lesbian, bisexual, transgender, and heterosexual student organization at Wabash College. 'shOUT aims to foster a safe and supportive environment for all members of the Wabash Community regardless of sexual orientation...[to] create an

---

[xxxi] Coincidentally at the moment of this writing a news report ran a story on the occurrence of same-sex prom dates across the nation. With the constant goading of the ACLU—the very personification of Openness—many more schools are allowing gay couples to attend prom ceremonies. The news story indicated most students do not seem to have a problem with it as more teenagers than ever before are coming out.

atmosphere of equality and acceptance both on and off the Wabash College campus.

What does the GLBT, official gay campus groups, pride demonstrations and rainbow paraphernalia really signify? Are times really that good that we have the luxury of investing a lot of it to bedroom behavior, which, quite truthfully, has moved out of the private bedroom and into public realms? What does it mean to be part of official sex clubs? What does the land have to gain from homosexual liberalism other than another "minority" to accept and Heaven forbid same-sex marriages? Ponder, wont you if homosexuals can demonstrate for a more homophilic environment because, say, they feel undervalued by society, then can heterosexuals who interpret their traditional and evolutionary principles as threatened express not the same remonstrance? Unlike gay members of academia, conservative and classical professors often draw a barrage of criticism as chauvinist, insecure relics. Since straight people are closed in their preferences then, it is argued, they are in need of education. They need to be made aware of the various alternative sexes. Perhaps the rise in gay pride serves a dual purpose:

- Gay pride builds the esteem of homosexuals, insuring them that they are o.k. and normal

- It makes others open to gayness, helping them to see that gay people are normal despite being alternative.

From another stance, if gay activism strives for civil equality by "interrogating" heterosexuality, then it plays the zero-sum game of whatever I win, you lose. According to Ms. Patai, this strategy is doomed if for no other reason than causing the overwhelming majority of people to steadfastly stay straight "while feeling nothing but estrangement from (if not ridicule for) the sort of feminists who tell them sternly they shouldn't be doing what they are doing, much less consider it 'natural' and enjoyable."[78]

In a very real sense the homosexual revolution may do more for hetero machismo as straight men work to keep from being mistaken gay. Some may call this effort insecurity on the part of the "straight" (they always say straight with incredulity) men. They may be correct. But in light of progressive academia's penchant for reinterpreting friendships like Sherlock Holmes and Dr. Watson, Bruce Wayne and Dick Grayson, Abe Lincoln and Joshua Speed, Bert and Ernie, Lone Ranger and Tonto, (and even Cagney and Lacey) to name a few, the effort is not unfounded. It is an understandable case of cause and effect, if you will.

Taped to the office door of one theater professor was a pride bumper sticker that announced in brightly assorted colors "Acceptance, not just tolerance". Other 'out' encouragement includes catchphrases like "We're here! We're queer!," "I'm not gay but my partner is"; the dedication to heterophobia, and such a popular cause as health: "Prevent AIDS. Aim for the chin." A rebellion that brandishes banners inscribed with bromides, wrote an intellect, is not a very convincing nor very inspiring sight.[79]

How and by what right can a man make another accept him? Contrary to the women's movements' and adjacent gay-lesbian-bisexual-transgender-asexual-polygimous-incestual-beastialogy-fetish-straight sex movement's frequent comparisons to the African-American Civil Rights Movement they are not birds of the same feather flocking together. The 1960 Civil Rights Movement is dissimilar on many grounds.

> In its early days almost all the significant leaders, in spite of tactical and temperamental differences, relied on the Declaration of Independence and the Constitution. They could charge whites not only with the most monstrous injustices but also with contradicting their own most sacred principles. The blacks were the true Americans in demanding the equality that belongs to them as human being by natural and political right. This stance implied a firm conviction of the truth of the principles of natural right and of their fundamental efficacy within the Constitutional tradition,

which, although tarnished, tends in the long run toward fulfilling those principles. They therefore worked through Congress, the Presidency, and, above all, the judiciary.[80]

Another flaw with the unfair comparison to African-Americans is that one's race and ethnicity is not a matter of one's choice. The person cannot contribute to the natural color of his skin—he is white, yellow, black, olive, and can do very little to permanently alter it. Nor can one customize his blood heritage—if he be of Indian, Scottish, Mexican, German ancestry, then that is what he is. It is a fixed genetic composite. Further, every case, though surgical advances can lend a changing knife, one will live and die as the gender one was born. These attributes are natural. To argue that gays and lesbians are entitled to special civil rights because they are a (questionable?) minority is to argue that teenagers deserve special civil recognition because premarital sex (and consequent pregnancies) are not generally encouraged; or that cousins who have intercourse (and in some cases marry and reproduce) are entitled to special civil rights because incest is also not highly regarded. In fact society is prejudiced against it.

Alternative sexual behavior is not really akin to dark skin, slitty eyes, or a certain ethnic cognomen. A bigot hating all twelve people sharing the same subway car does not automatically make those dozen folk friends or allies. I do not believe sexual orientation should become a matter of civil rights to be decided by legislation. The gay agenda is trying to enter into the making of the laws. In *Heterophobia* the author comments on the seemingly odd change in liberal activism's "desire for intervention."[xxxii] Compared to yesteryear's

---

[xxxii] *Heterophobia*, 196. Patai believes this ideology is so nurtured today out of naivete and actual experience with censorship and totalitarian systems. Because young people have grown up enjoying individual liberties as effortlessly as one blinks his eye-lids, there is a noticeable un-appreciation, an indifference to them. For example, she finds it shocking to meet students who, apparently indifferent to their right to free speech, "support censoring speech and behavior even in an academic setting—always assuming, of course, that this will above all affect *others,* and not themselves"(197).

activists, today's liberals are principally concerned with sexual behavior and far less concerned with "true economic and political reform."[81]

More, regardless of whether a gay gene actually exists (which medical science has not concluded), homosexual behavior can be guarded, controlled, hidden. It is an issue of choice. I cannot hide my blackness which includes skin pigmentation, physical features, certain mannerisms. Anyone can tell, from a distance, that I am a black man. The same can not always be safely said of a gay person though changing times are permitting more and more of that persuasion to sport gear that typically signifies gay awareness. (Also, many fashions that were once typically gay are commonly sported by straight people; e.g., men wearing ear-rings or lots of jewelry, women wearing pants or short haircuts or tattoos, et cetera.) There exists the matter of public and private exhibit. Ask why they should have to hide themselves and you might as well ask the same of "kissing cousins."

And if it is biological, a gay gene, what then? In early July 2000, Drs. J. Craig Venter and Francis Collins revealed that together, they have mapped the genetic code of human beings. All 3.1 billion biochemical letters of human DNA have been deciphered. Yet, with over 85 percent of the sequencing known, not one combination of letters spells out homosexuality. Still, let us entertain this fiction. Why the fuss over homosexuality? (Because the overwhelming majority of people feel it is an acquired disease not only unhealthy but also morally and ethically corrupt.) And what do others say? (Others say that some people are naturally born that way and should not have to conform to society's wishes that they be straight or normal.) Thus we can all agree that being gay is, at least, negatively perceived. The big question is whether or not gay activism would benefit from the discovery of a gay gene.

Part of my perspective toward the possibility of a gay gene is well illustrated by the movie *Gattaca* (1997). Set in the "not-too-distant future," procreation as we know it will produce second rate citizens (called "invalids" or "de*gene*rates") to those offspring conceived in the laboratories (called "valids"). Leaving nothing to chance, valids are a genetically engineered breed of near perfect human beings minus all the natural imperfections of baldness, high blood pressure, glaucoma, heart disease, flat feet, alcoholism, obesity, et cetera, et cetera. The scientists leave nothing to chance. And, if a gay gene does exist, how improbable is it that research for its cure will not soon be underway? If given technological foresight what parents would allow their child to be born with a propensity towards homosexuality? "We were biologically meant to give birth to more people. Not being able to relate normally to a member of the opposite sex is some kind of error," Dr. Laura explained in an interview. "I do not see that as insulting at all. It is a statement of biological fact."[82] Now, you decide, which side of the argument is best helped by the gay gene theory?

As best as I can interpret it, the issue over gay rights is one of hurt personal feelings (not completely incomprehensible) and a lack of general comfort. The matter is, not about constitutional rights. It is about political demands. The Constitution does not promise comradery or respect for blacks, Greeks, Jews, the physically challenged (a PC term in place of the word handicapped), whites, or Catholics. What it does guarantee, wrote Bloom, is "the protection of the rights of individual human beings. This has not proved to be enough, however, to what is perhaps by now a majority of Americans." In an earlier section he wrote that the equal protection of the laws did not protect a man from contempt and hatred as a Jew, an Indian, or a Black. In the same vein, Dr. Martin Luther King, Jr. said that the law can not make a man **like** you but it can have him treat you like a man, that is to say, equally and with a measure of civility and dignity.

The ebb of male institutions is by no means a mere fluke, a testimony that all things come to an end with time. More than time, it was legislation and lawsuits that damned former bastions of maleness while simultaneously creating and protecting female-only interests. In the end we have what can reasonably be called a disproportionate balance of purposeful institutions and agencies. In America, in addition to the hundreds of coeducation colleges and universities, there are well over 60 women's colleges and only 4 men's colleges. Unlike the nation's 79 all female colleges," wrote one magazine, "all male schools often draw snickers as chauvinist relics."[83] Am I to gather that Wabash, Morehouse, Deep Springs, and Hampton-Sydney College all pose a threat to our society?

Understanding Openness' intent to make all fractionated audiences one, it would make more sense that we should see Mrs. Wollstonecraft's dream of public co-educational reality. Which is to say that schools—all of which only admitted boys—would accommodate and instruct young men and women. In fact public co-education is the norm of the day. Many people are surprised to learn that a men's college still exists. Still, how are we to explain the great disproportionate number of women's colleges to men's colleges in the present? The most common reply is that in order to gain more parity in our society there is a necessity for women to learn and fellowship together absent of the intimidation of young men. Do not also boys and men grow stronger, more fruitful even, in the company of other men? To the unfortunate irony of Openness, men's fellowship is seen as "the 'ol boys club" (with that nasty connotation). Men's fellowship is seen as a threat to women instead of a benefit to the men themselves. The pervading rhetoric supposes every man in a position of command will soon become abusive and domineering. The Greeks applaud a positive male energy—Zeus energy—that has accepted authority.[84] Therein is the logic—male institutions and activities are sexist and impede the progress of society—and therein is where I find fault.

Are we to believe that unmanly things will propel the world to equity? Will a dominant matriarchy make right every wrong and produce total parity? Maybe Freud's deduction of female's penis envy is not crazy or misogynist. After all, the general rhetoric of today's "Sexual Harassment Industry" is that the phallus is powerful and oppressive. If real men are to purge themselves they must throw away their masculinity and just be "human". Presumably humans don't have penises—just like women.

Gender-socialists, which is to say girl-partisans as they are genuinely anti-male, see masculinity as problematic and dangerous, ergo, boys (quite unlike girls) are deviant and dangerous, and in need of re-masculinization; better yet, de-masculinization. Mrs. Sommers noted as much:

> Unfortunately, many educators have become persuaded that there is truth in the relentlessly repeated proposition that masculinity per se is the cause of violence. Beginning with the factual premise that most violence is perpetrated by men, they move hastily (and fallaciously) to the proposition that maleness is the leading cause of violence. By this logic, every little boy is a potential harasser and batterer.[85]

The truth of the matter behind gender-socialists' propaganda is that "in American society, healthy, normal young men (which is to say, the overwhelming majority) don't batter, rape, or terrorize women; they respect them and treat them as friends."[86]

Earlier we examined self-hatred in feminized men. Now we turn to the opposite sex where there is evidence of a similar mentality. In all the talk about gender studies femininity is rarely discussed or questioned, and when it is, it is only done so in juxtaposition, in challenging masculinity. The womb is never praised despite the substance in the saying *the hand that rocks the cradle rules the world.* Such course studies see female virtues as not virtues but social and demeaning constructs while male attributes, primarily the phallus, are analyzed for their "hidden" destructiveness. Although the majority of contemporary psychologists debunk Freud's theory of penis envy, to play Devil's advocate for a moment, allow me to boldly assert that lesbian feminists hate themselves for not being men and, thus, seek to androgynize—humanize—the world. Their unreasonable mentality reminds me of the Aesop's Fable, "The Fox and the Sour Grapes." Drs. Patai and Sommers are not the only clear-eyed feminists. In 1934, British writer Katharine Burdekin published *Proud Man* in which an android remarks of England circa 1930s:

Naturally a female dominance would make the race no happier, nor bring it a whit nearer to humanity. The privilege would merely be reversed, and possibly it would be more oppressive and more cruel.[87]

The numbers are too telling. In 2000 there are only four small men's colleges left in the nation and each is constantly pestered by progressive causes, to—you guessed it—go coed. What are the dangers of single-sex education? More, what is so destructive and unhealthy about single-sex education for boys? In the fall of 1997 (my entrance year in college) two military colleges—Virginia Military Institute (VMI) and South Carolina's Citadel—were forced into enrolling female cadets. In the span of my high school senior year the number of men's colleges dropped by two. The U.S. Supreme Court's decision rendered the military colleges' all male enrollments unconstitutional and, therefore, illegal on the majority opinion (written by Justice Ruth Ginsburg) that they "perpetuate the legal, social and economic inferiority of women."[88] I think it would have been an entirely different matter if the schools purported to accept all—all!—applicants in which the unjustified rejection of an applicant would be grounds for investigation. But VMI and the Citadel, from the first freshman to the class of 1997, advertised themselves as military colleges for men. Shannon Faulkner, the young woman who caused the disturbance and subsequent integration at the Citadel in 1995, applied under false pretenses (she knew she was not a young man) and did not last more than a few days before subsequently dropping out. After all that hoopla she drops out. The following fall, four young women enrolled. In the fall of late 1999, one of them, Jeanie Mentavlos, quit the school but not before settling a sexual harassment lawsuit for an undisclosed sum.

According to *Marine Corps Times*, Miss Mentavlos "quit in frustration" because she could no longer endure a semester of being "shoved and kicked and [having] her clothes set on fire by her fellow cadets. Other cadets said the harassment was no greater that what men experience at the formerly all-male school."[89] Looking at the situation, it seems women enter formerly all-male colleges under special situations and leave likewise. Regarding VMI it just so happened that Justice Clarence Thomas' son was attending the school at the time. Under the rules, Justice Thomas was excluded from the decision-making. (That probably did not amount to much since he is often regarded across political parties as the Supreme Court Juror.)

In a situation closer to home for the author, the last time the faculty and trustee board of Wabash College voted on its all-male status was in 1992. The student body is **still** single-sex. The greater part of the campus is Greek and all the living units competitively participate on varsity and intramural sports. For several straight years, the *Princeton Review* rated Wabash the number one "jock school." But the tradition and pride goes deeper. Instructors who represent character, scholarship, and the gentleman are admired. From *The Wabash Commentary* ("Manhood in America"):

> Wabash is blessed with several such mentors. The sensible student will seek them out, for being in the presence of a *real* man is a rare luxury nowadays…To ask a question and receive an honest reply. To be told when one is behaving foolishly, and be encouraged to do the honorable thing. Such men are rare indeed and are rightly cherished.
>
> Wabash has a moral duty to hire more professors who will serve as paternal mentors—confident, out-going men who will challenge students to reach their highest level of personal development.[90]

Mr. Bly hit the proverbial nail on the head when he said, "All the great cultures except ours preserve and have lived with images of this positive male energy."[91]

Why is there such a willingness to deem predominately male organizations bad and, therefore, in need of change either through "proportionality" or closing? Are men to have no place, activity, preference, or institution for them nowadays without fear of lawsuits over accusations of unconstitutionality or sexual discrimination?

Efforts have been made to re-experiment with single-sex programs for boys but

> they find groups such as the National Organization for Women and the American Civil Liberties Union poised to oppose them. In 1989, threats of lawsuits from both organizations prevented the Detroit public schools from proceeding with plans for all-male academies for at-risk urban youths. When schools in Dade County, Florida, were considering establishing two all-male classes for underachieving boys, the U.S. Department of Education's Office of Civil Rights blocked them.[92]

We come now to a crucial section of a child's journey to adulthood—rites of passage. Nowadays, though, there is very little in the way of formal rites of passages. Boys and girls grow old (note I did not say grow up) without traditional definitive passages. I think this void in child development accounts for much of the trouble, cynicism, and anger we see in American youth? American teenagers don't know where they are going and neither do their parents, hence the name, Generation X. Who knows what to make of them? Are they children, young adults, adults, or just people? Other than age, there appears to be scant that distinguishes a child and teenager from adults and elders. How are boys and girls to know when they have culturally become men and women when absolutist ideologies permeate, mitigate, and obliterate traditional passage? Since I am writing about disappearing masculinity, I shall focus solely on the topic of young men.

Generally speaking, boys in this nation are deprived of a clear ritual administered by older men which signifies their transition from boyhood to manhood. We have lost our rituals. Many people affiliated with Wabash, like to think of the College as a rites of passage of sorts in these our contemporary, progressive times. "Alumni do not reminisce about exams;" wrote Mr. Rarey, "they praise professors who taught them to be men."[93]

To effectively deride men and masculinity, progressive academics have a penchant for "analyzing" and challenging the male member. They generalize and polarize the alpha male. When feminists and philosophers attack the relevancy of the phallus as a definer of man they might do well to evaluate the circumstances of which they were contributory. Could it be the disappearance of fraternal rituals and instruction have left Generation X-ers to ground their claim to manliness (if they do so at all) in the fact that they possess a penis and females do not? After all, since the Industrial Revolution, the bonding time between the father and the son has decreased. That instruction and constantly visible model has been removed because of competing obligations to go out and work and keep face as provider and protector. When feminist rhetoric enters the picture the matter is befuddled more. Therefore, as superficial as it may be, members of Generation X are not totally at fault in staking manhood to the penis. This is where the culture stands as gender specifics are constantly blurred. The organ and the psychology that comes along with owning one (along with the Y-chromosome and testosterone) are what separate boys from girls.[xxxiii]

Where have our rites of passage, our models gone? Better, why have such rites left?[xxxiv] Many debatable factors may shed some light on the present deficiency of the father. Among them are whether he is a feminized, absentee or deadbeat dad; or perhaps the impact of de-emphasis and discouragement of masculinity. Another factor is the scarcity of fathers, father-figures, and visible models or exemplars in the

---

[xxxiii] Interestingly, codpieces were commonly worn from the 15th to the 17th century; first as the practical predecessor to the modern zipper and some time later as fashionable credentials. (Somewhere along the line, however, women took to wearing codpieces perhaps as a sort of challenge or mockery to the definition of man, thinking satirically, If *this* is what makes a man, then I, a woman, can be a man as often and for as long as is convenient. Thus, the critiquing and mockery of the penis' significance goes way back.)

[xxxiv] To quote Christina Sommers: It all began with the assumption that our 'patriarchal' society conspires to favor boys and to keep girls down (99).

way of John Wayne, Ernest Hemingway, Norman Rockwell, John F. Kennedy, Michael Jordan, Generals Patton, MacArthur, and Powell, Charles Atlas, Malcolm X, Muhammad Ali, Theodore Roosevelt (who carried a big stick), Sidney Portier, Charles Lindbergh, Mahatma Gahndi, Dr. Martin Luther King, Jr., or Cary Cooper. Sociologist David Blankenhorn believes the father figure is central to healthy development of masculinity. "There are exceptions, of course. But here is the rule. Boys raised by traditionally masculine fathers generally do not commit crimes. Fatherless boys commit crimes."[94]

Apostle Paul said it most excellently in I Corinthians 13:11: *When I was a child I spake as a child, I understood as a child, I thought as a child but when I became a man I put away childish things.* Without training there is no **direct** guidance into the ways of manhood and citizenship (e.g., chivalry, gentlemanly conduct, self-defense). Consequently, the country (and women) ends up with old teenagers instead of young adults. They have, as I once heard professor Cornel West refer to America, "grown big and grown old without having grown up!"[xxxv] Plato advanced a similar belief, stressing the necessity of humility before greatness. Any man needs to have been a slave before he can be a good master—a slave to the laws, the gods, and honored senior members of the community. As it stands, disregarding puberty, the only real cultural sign that a boy is becoming a man is the mandatory selective service registration for 18-year old males. Some people, including myself, think these forty years of emasculation have made us more game to reconsider initiations and meeting the Wild Man.

There are a few cultures in America that still maintain rites of passage for its youth, namely Native Americans. Many Native American nations acknowledge and test the maturity and competence of its respective boys (and girls). The Nations do not politicize and disregard the healthful nourishing male power. The black Church is always talking about the

---

[xxxv] A speech delivered at Northern Illinois University in February 1998.

need—understandably so—for male role models. In 1997 the Million Man March was the African-American community's response to declining manhood. Billed as a Day of Atonement the march initiated what will hopefully prove an effective call to black men to be strong responsible citizens and caretakers.

The last assault on maleness I will address concerns the deterioration of the traditional family. For a time it seemed the father, having been interrupted by the Industrial Revolution and wars was beginning to be re-included in the newborn's development. More men were being encouraged to attend parenthood workshops, to accompany his wife during the delivery, and to actively interact with the infant (the first two years are critical). Now, however, it appears to me the man's role is seen as useless or moot beyond consummation. Prefacing this was the de-emphasis on marriage. The women's movement has long regarded marriage a crippling male invention and advocated refraining from it. Some women believed sacrifice of motherhood was a small price to pay for equal opportunities. But, why sacrifice motherhood, changing times asked? Unwed mothers eventually became less of a family embarrassment. If all the pregnant girls in my schools had been sent off to live with the aunt or cousin across town, a great deal of hall traffic would have been lessened.

Openness wants to make things as indiscriminate as possible; making what is good for the geese equally so for the gander. Hence if men can have casual sex, if men can retain their name, if men talk, brag even, of conquests, and do this and that then why can't women, goes the argument? (The feminine virtue of modesty I think has retired to antiquity.)

While many a child has been spawned by deadbeat fathers wasn't there a time when emphasis on marriage was a sign of owning up to responsibility? More than several times have I heard mothers and pregnant women declare their independence of a man. Ask what about the father and you will get one of the two responses: Who? He ain't nobody—this is my baby. Or, He can be a part of the baby's life (if he chooses). The former remark is selfish stupidity, the latter a shameful compromise. "I don't need a man!" is quite synonymous with "I am woman, hear me roar!" It's the same catchphrase—just a different decade.

Research and data back the importance of the father to a boy's sound development. This should be common sense but since no Ph.D is offered in 'common sense' it is lost on many academics and on most experts of gender studies. Citing the U. S. Bureau of the Census and social scientific studies, Mrs. Sommers, informs readers that it is literal separation from their fathers that puts boys at higher risks of juvenile delinquency and anti-social violence. As the phenomenon of fatherlessness has increased, she says, so has violence.[xxxvi]

What is to be made of this I-don't-need-a-man attitude? Why is there such angst to the father being around? I personally know this to be true in many urban areas including my own. For the sake of illustration I will use celebrity exemplars. The '90s woman—career minded, business savvy, college educated, independent—has come to realize that despite societal constructs she still has a desire to bear children. As if to compromise between the feminist ideas of womanhood and self-reliance and her biological clock, many female celebrities have turned to adoption or "hiring" a reproducer. The deterioration of the traditional family module is breaking down into two parts: the single parent- and the homosexual parents-home.

Why is holy matrimony so passe? When did this attitude visibly take root? Could a lack of expectations through the condoning of "free love" be to blame?[95]

Apparently, reader, it was only a myth that the ideal basic family consisted of a mother, father, 2.5 children (and a pet). Jodie Foster and Madonna, for example, had men to naturally conceive child with no intent of long term relationship. Also mythical was the basic composite of

---

[xxxvi] See also Senator Patrick Moyihan's 1965 project, *The Negro Family: The Case for National Action* (U.S. Department of Labor); also chance the following website for population information and statistics: http://www.census.gov/population/socdemo.

parents as man and woman. Tolerance for open gayness is making it more acceptable for gay couples to adopt children or retain them in the case of a divorce.

In addition to the military, the other critical sphere that ought to resist the current unnatural trend is the reproduction of family. Medical advances and perversion of law have changed the family as we know it. No one has a right to augment the dependency of procreation on the duality of the sexes. That was the one unchangeable glitch, sacrifice, drawback, axiom, and maxim, of homosexuality.[xxxvii]

Melissa Etheridge and her female lover successfully had two children through generous sperm donor and folk singer David Crosby. In the exclusive *Rolling Stones* interview co-mother of the "twenty-first century family" Ms. Etheridge said, "I know that because of the procreation of our species that it was man and woman, and that's the way it was all built. But two loving parents—that's all a kid needs. Two men, two women, a man and a woman, whatever. It's amazing what loving parents can do." Whatever? No, not whatever—parents should not be whatever. A baby will benefit from loving parents, having the polarity of father and mother, in addition to surrounding institutions, e.g., a denominated church, extended family or close friends, community center, school, et cetera. Homosexuality does not maintain the duality of the sexes, hence barring procreation and forfeiting parenthood. Period. Not whatever.

Here is the case of Baby Terry. Baby Terry, an infant boy, within the past year or so became the adopted son of proud poppas Terry Miller and Dan Savage. Like Rudyard Kipling's abandoned prince, Baby Terry will probably grow up with an 'open' concept of parents and family; a mommy

---

[xxxvii] The power of modern science is transforming and expanding avenues of human procreation. The traditional mother and father role is growing more and more optional or moot. Several laboratories around the world are experimenting with human cloning. Julie Cypher said in Rolling Stones Magazine (March 3, 2000), "There are single women going to sperm banks, lesbians going to sperm banks, gay guys going to surrogates."

and daddy, he may reason is the same as a mommy and mommy is the same as a daddy and daddy.

Maybe it's a good thing, mused David Crosby, for a lot of families to see that this is not something strange. Not strange? If not strange Mr. Crosby, then what are a lot of families to conclude of you fertilizing the eggs of one lesbian for the purpose of she and her lover having a "natural" family? To argue that these twin padres or alternative parents are no different than say a grandparent or aunt taking the place of guardian is erroneous on the sole ground that the grandparent or aunt is not mommy's/daddy's bed partner.

The absence of father figures has made its way into the gauge of mainstream America—television. Even earlier, though, comics in the 1920s and 1930s such as "Blondie and Dagwood" depicted men weak and foolish, a concept that carried over into animated cartoons.[96] In the mid-1990s, Vice President Dan Qualye criticized Candice Bergman's television character Murphy Brown for bearing a child out of wedlock. As it happened, Murphy Brown was a middle-aged career woman (TV journalist). The VP, in turn, was criticized and ridiculed by entertainers and liberals for worrying about a fictitious character instead of non-fictitious pressing issues. A couple seasons later "Thelma" and "Grace Under Fire" aired. These prime time family sitcoms were slightly different in that they depicted single mothers trying to manage children, work, and a love life after the separating from their husbands. Emphasis was on Grace and Thelma making it. Furthermore in these shows, several male figures (e.g., an uncle, grandfather, neighbor, co-worker) fill the role of surrogate fathers. None of this was apparent in "Murphy Brown." On a witty note, "Seinfeld" had a running sketch where the colloquially used word "bastard" was mistakenly applied to an actual baby born without a father. The embarrassed mother freaks from shame when she hears Elaine innocently coo, "Aren't you a *cute* little bastard?"

When a father is included in sitcoms he usually comes off very foolish as in incompetent, bumbling, devious, absent-minded. He is an entertaining clown who everyone gets over on. Instead of making the father a strong, wise, credible breadwinner (who has a sense of humor) we are given someone who is basically a slapstick figurehead, a mere contributor of sperm and name. All the poplar network family shows have paternal idiot savants, e.g., "Home Improvement", "The Simpsons", "The Family Guy", "Everybody Loves Raymond", "Roseanne", "Happily Ever After", and "Married With Children". Bly (who by now sounds like a pseudo-psychologist) nicely suggests this attack on masculine integrity, this "undermining" of Zeus energy by many young Hollywood writers is a sort of revenge on the remote father.[97] Look through all the laughter and the clear impression is that (TV) fathers are jokes; no one to be taken seriously. In reality, which is anyplace as far removed of television cameras as possible, "widespread fatherlessness is not a conundrum but a personal and social tragedy."[98]

I am still not all together sure of what feminism means or what feminism is supposed to stand for, even. But to judge by the current hysteria with sexual harassment lawsuits, gender equity, speech codes, and women's studies on everything from Shakespeare to computer science being touted and fanned *under the banner* of feminism, I do not think it a good thing. Carol Tavris wants to believe we still need feminism, but, she added, a different kind of feminism for the new century. All the same, a feminized culture will not for long keep man's nature knitted up.[99] American males—adolescents and adults—are in trouble and we are shouting, "Iron John, Iron John!"

39 *Heterophobia,* 41.

40 Ibid, 149.

41 *The War Against Boys,* 60-61.

42 "Interview: Jacques Barzun," *The Women's Quartley,* Autumn 2000, 18-20.

43 Ibid, 51.

44 "Men's Losses in Collegiate Athletics," [March 18, 2000], www.wrestlingusa.com/titlenine.html.

45 Lena Williams, "N.C.A.A. Reports Movement Toward Equality of the Sexes," *New York Times,* November 1999.

46 Brendan I. Koerner, "Where the Boys Aren't," *U.S. News & World Report,* 8 February 1999, 46-55

47 "Where the Boys Aren't," 48.

48 Ibid.

49 *The War Against Boys,* 51.

50 Kimberly Schuld"Why Would a Women's Group Complain?" [March 18, 2000] http://www.wrestlingusa.com/titlenine.html.

51 Dale Anderson, "If you are a wrestler, read this and give it to your parents," *Wrestling U.S.A. Magazine,* 35, no. 1, 15 September 1999, 21.

52 *Tragedy,* section 13, 86.

53 "Men's Losses in Collegiate Athletics," [March 18, 2000] http://www.wrestlingusa.com/titlenine.html..

54 Ibid.

55 Matthew Rarey, "Manhood in America," *The Wabash Commentary* (February/March 1999), 12.

56 "Where the Boys Aren't," 50.

57 Kathleen S. Berger and Ross A. Thompson, authors *The Developing Person: Through Childhood and Adolescence,* 4th ed, (New York: Worth Publishers,1995), 529.

58 *Heterophobia,* 11.

[59] "Why Would a Women's Group Complain About Title IX?" http://www.wrestlingusa.com/titlenine.html.

[60] *War Against Boys,* 133.

[61] *The Developing Person,* 537-39.

[62] *Iron John,* 2.

[63] *Heterophobia,* 118.

[64] Marilyn Frye, author of "Willful Virgins: *Essays in Feminism,*" 1976-1992, 132, quoted by Patai, *Heterophobia,* 144.

[65] *Heterophobia,* 148.

[66] *Closing,* 30.

[67] John Stoltenberg, author of "Refusing To Be A Man: Essays on Sex and Justice," 1990, 88, quoted by Patai, *Heterophobia,* 151.

[68] *Iron John,* 2.

[69] Ibid, 2-3.

[70] Crompton, 3.

[71] John Stoltenberg, *End of Manhood: A Book For Men of Conscience,* 1993, 211, quoted by Patai, *Heterophobia,* 150.

[72] *End of Manhood,* 7-8, quoted by Patai, *Heterophobia,* 151-52.

[73] *Closing,* 101.

[74] *Iron John,* 6.

[75] Ibid, 6.

[76] Deborah Sterns, author of "Gendered Sexuality: The Privilege of Sex and Gender in Sexual Orientation," *NWSA [National Women's Studies Association] Journal* 7, no. 1 (Spring 1995), 8-29, quoted by Patai, *Heterophobia,* 147.

[77] www.home.cc.unmanitoba.ca/wyatt/tv-characters.com

[78] *Heterophobia,* 147.

[79] *The New Left,* 30.

[80] *Closing,* 33.

81 *Heterophobia,* 196.

82 Jeanne McDowell. "Preacher, Teacher, Nag: Dr. Laura Speaks her Mind," *Time,* 3 July 2000, 59.

83 David Whitman, "The Masculine Mystique: Wabash College, one of a dying breed," *US News & World Report,* 8 February 1999,55.

84 *Iron John,* 22.

85 *War Against Boys,* 63.

86 Ibid.

87 Heterophobia, *207.*

88 *United States v. Virginia,* 116.S Ct 2264, June 26, 1996.

89 "Citadel Settles Lawsuit," *Marine Corps Times,* 1999.

90 "Manhood in America," 14.

91 *Iron John,*23.

92 *War Against Boys,* 171.

93 "Manhood in America," 14.

94 David Blankenhorn, *Fatherless America,* quoted by Sommers, *War Against Boys,* 130.

95 Sir Thomas More, *Utopia: and History of King Richard III.,* ed. Alexander Young (Boston: Hilliard, Gray, and Co., 1834), 129.

96 *Iron John,* 23.

97 Ibid.

98 *War Against Boys,* 132.

99 Steven Drukman, "Danger! Masculinity Crisis!" *Out,* February 2000, 50.

OPEN WARFARE

▼

I would rather fail in a cause that will ultimately triumph than to triumph in a cause that will ultimately fail.

—Woodrow Wilson

THREAT TO PATRIOTISM

American society is yielding to the infinite wails of what I believe basically amount to expressions of discomfort and hurt feelings. America is being made to feel guilty for everything under the gaping ozone layer. Worse, popular discontent is justifiable. What is the basis of justifiable popular discontent? Principally, that social inequality or revolving door of lawsuits, complaints, unhappiness, and irritations. This is a problem.

This problem is only furthered by the solution which is problematic in itself because the reformers are part of the problem. Lady Liberty is receiving emotional and legal therapy from the same intellectual coup evoking the guilty conscience in the first place. Is it not ill fated for the lover to take advice from the batterer? And it won't be easy reversing or even approaching the situation because any solution with elements of the social problem itself will ineffectively treat the trouble. It is futile to ask the Judge to arrest socialism when socialism is the Judge. He is not going to arrest himself! It is a vicious cycle. Proponents of the Openness ideology see their emotional therapy more in the light of intellectual enlightenment, "making us aware…" and "making us open to…." That feelings of guilt occur with some people just happens to be a side effect. But these guises—speech codes, sensitivity training, unity, big brother surveillance, "awareness" forums, false volunteerism and enlightenment—do not fool me.

The intellectual coup of Openness can loosely be tagged the liberal Left. By the droves they dwell in the ivory tower. These members of academia are in large part responsible for the spread of Openness. From what I have seen and gathered from college workshops, summer programs, campus visits, and, of course, being a current undergraduate, the academics is mostly comprised of professors who predominately come off as nostalgic hippies or the anxious Left.

From a more panoramic perspective, the movement, like any other, has its diversity of motives. Written three decades past and in direct response to the student "rebellions" (author's quotations) of the 1960s and early 1970s, Ayn Rand's analysis of the rebels still hold true for today's voices of politically correct, gay-rights, cultural, and socialist activism.

> There are the little shysters of the intellect who have found a gold mine in modern philosophy, who delight in arguing for argument's sake and stumping opponents by means of ready-to-wear paradoxes—there are the little role-players who fancy themselves as heroes and enjoy defiance for the sake of defiance—there are the nihilists who, moved by a profound hatred, seek nothing but destruction for the sake of destruction—there are the hopeless dependents who seek to 'belong' to any crowd that would have them….[100]

Social reformers like the luring Left are not alone in enfeebling patriotism. The Moloch we call Hollywood contributes substantially to the "lack of's" we observe in mainstream America through contemporary movies that hype the lack of self-control (needless violence; players display no cognitive ability to entertain alternative methods); the lack of conscience ('casual sex' debunks any pretensions of societal angst over promiscuity); the lack of intelligence or articulation (dominance by monosyllabic words; e.g., *Pulp Fiction*, holds the dubious honor for film with the most usage of "f--" and *9 Months* opens with Hugh Grant screaming "F--!" five consecutive times);[xxxviii] the lack of positive and constructive on-screen and off-screen characters; and the lack of explicitly patriotic works.

American youth are learning that ethnocentrism—pride in self and pride in nation—is more of a flaw, a relic of superpower arrogance than anything else. The most paramount ingredient in and of Openness is its heavily lectured display of tolerance. *Be more tolerant! Exercise more tolerance! You are too intolerant!*, they say. Translation: you are too insensitive. While "tolerance" is dogmatically pushed, it is really "acceptance" that is expected. Acceptance is about the only expectation held by Openness.

The Left confuses the distinction between tolerance and acceptance. Tolerance and acceptance are not synonymous. Briefly, tolerance is an act of habituation; a behavior of willed courtesy and perhaps even civility against personal preference. On the other hand, reader, acceptance, is signification of agreement, likeness. Acceptance says *I support you 100%*. 'Accepting' something you do not accept can be upsetting, nerve wrecking, and frustrating. The world does not "belong" to any of us; therefore we must try to co-exist as peacefully as possible. Civilization functions on this—give and take—requiring that we exhibit mutual courtesy and respect.

May I be permitted to tolerate someone without fully accepting him? More, can those grounds of non-acceptance be in regard to his ideals, philosophy, his habits, pet peeves, political affiliation, his appearances, social status, et cetera? Of course I may be permitted to not be sociable

---

xxxviii I find it amazing that the James Bond series still manages to work within a PG-13 rating.

with any one I choose. It is called freedom of association. Anything to the contrary would be forced association. In this great big world of people and ever advancing machines, I think it is naïve to expect individuals to agree with every other individual, group, existing thing or social invention. Openness is naïve and the influence of its pervading naivete is dangerous.

To return to Openness in the classrooms, I am convinced that students have adopted an outfit of self-mitigation through acts of naked tolerance, i.e., absolute tolerance. This rejection of pride and self is constructed through the derision of ethnocentrism. American youth are coming to understand they are the citizens of the real Evil Empire, that our founding fathers are no more different than fascists or dictators, that our government system is not a democracy, that democracy, by the way, is not the best form of government, and that natural citizenship to America obligates—obligates!—them to accept foreign ideologies and foreign classmates. Forced fraternity and rigged associations are shams. They are acts of injustice. (To what?) To liberty.

> The study of history and of culture teaches that all the world was mad in the past; men always thought they were right, and that led to wars, persecutions, slavery, xenophobia, racism, and chauvinism. The point is not to correct the mistakes and really be right; rather it is not to think you are right at all.[101]

Could this be the reason why counter-culture backlash is such the staple of open dialogues? If not, then it most surely is the impression many students walk away with. It is the impression I am left with. Mr. Bloom said: "relativism has extinguished the real motive of education, the search for a good life."[102] What I believe many of my peers absorb from all of this is an enlightened disdain for the American half of their hyphenated Americanism, and a naked, i.e., indiscriminate acceptance of the other. The acceptance is naked or blind because: first, the student is unable to formulate, let alone support, his reasons for accepting the non-Western,[xxxix] and secondly, because the professor's pedagogy goes unchallenged.

The threat to patriotism extends beyond the classroom, beyond academia. Campuses are, from many perspectives, a microcosm of the 'real world.' At the core of America's existence are the principles of basic natural rights that are best phrased, "*We hold these truths to be self-evident that all men are created equal and endowed by their Creator with certain unalienable rights.*" We as a nation cling to the concept of liberty. Americans, and most other peoples of the Western world, believe freedom is not only the highest secular virtue but that it is ideal. Freedom is ideally illustrated and demonstrated by individualism, capitalism, and democracy. We hold these three constructs to be self-evident of the true meaning of freedom. Actor Charleton Heston once said during a speech

---

[xxxix] The same may be said of chauvinist ideals but at least here there is perhaps a line of exemplars, testimonials, and social influences. Put another way, the person has lived or experienced a way of life that lends credit to his belief system. Many times the difficulty in explaining our personal beliefs stem from it being what psychologist Jerome Bruner (*Acts of Meaning*) called an experience-near concept. That is, the experience or practice is so near, it is so much a part of our culture that it is somewhat difficult recognizing the behavior as anything other than 'common sense'; non-canonical. The other reason for one having difficulty in defending one's beliefs and behaviors is due to an absence of inoculation; he has rarely, if ever, had to logically support his actions. However, taking in something different—not experience-near—should not be as difficult to explain. For instance, I would expect that most people would find it nearly impossible to explain (in anatomical terms) how they walk or read text, but would probably have an easier time conveying a new dance step or a new speed-reading technique because they had to 'consciously' memorize and practice it. "Man," Hayek maintained, "certainly does not know all the rules which guide his actions in the sense that he is able to state them in words"(43) ergo we should not cease breathing because the positivist asks us to define its existence.

at a convention of Quixtar business owners and dreamers[xl], "The instinct for freedom seems to be part of the human nature."

To say the United States of America is an individualist country is like saying *Citizen Kane* is a black-and-white film; both are an understatement. Most U.S. citizens cannot imagine any other way of life than the freedom of life, liberty, and the pursuit of happiness. Generally speaking, this attitude begins to be sowed not long after a baby is born.[103] A study done by Morelli, Rogoff, Oppenheim, and Goldsmith (1992) investigated the sleeping arrangements of children in the U.S. and children in Guatemala. As reported in Pillemer's work, their data showed that 80% of U.S. babies slept in a separate room from their parents by 6 months of age. "In middle-class U.S. families, most parents apparently believe that children are born dependent and that autonomy must be encouraged beginning at an early age, even if the process of individualism is a stressful one. According to one U.S. mother, 'It was time to give him his own room...his own territory. That's the American way'"(Morelli et al., p. 604).

It was time to give him his own room...his own territory. That's the American way. Thus, we see that to strike out on our own, to be physically separate, to grow into self is, by and large, the general tendency of our culture to discourage dependence and develop an independent person.

[xl] Don't think it queer of me to refer to entrepreneurs and 'go-getters' as dreamers. Everything great starts with a dream or an idea. You might be surprised to learn how many people cannot even dream; they are beaten, cynical, passive, or, worst of all, nihilistic. The Quixtar business repeatedly stresses the value of dreaming and working to bring one's wildest dreams to fruition. Even more, three great contributors to this century expressed the import of the un-statistical or impracticality of dreams: Ralph Waldo Emerson said, "Nothing great was ever achieved without enthusiasm." Albert Einstein believed that imagination was more important than knowledge; and Dr. Martin Luther King, Jr.'s "I Have a Dream" speech is one of the most stirring speeches of our time. Therefore, reader, never stop dreaming. The person who ceases to dream, in all respects, has ceased living.

Individualism harnesses self-reliance and separation from ingroups (e.g., within a team one person is typically honored as the most valuable player and it is understood by the other team members that they need not also feel honored. As Andy Warhol quipped, "Everyone deserves to be famous for at least fifteen minutes."). The individualist can appropriately be called independent, idiocentric, or, even selfish. Above all else, however, the individualist embraces the 'I': *I am my own man; I am somebody; I am woman, hear me roar; I have rights; If it is to be, it is up to me.*

Perhaps the value and significance of the I-self will be better seen through juxtaposition with a collectivist perspective. The collectivist can appropriately be called interdependent and allocentric. By and large, people of a culture that adopts the collectivist perspective rarely, if ever, distinguish between personal and familial goals, and if a distinction is made, the familial goal supercedes the personal goal.[104] In collectivism "the experience is that of a we-self."[105] Probably the best example of the Eastern world's anti-individualism is Asian culture. "Chinese language also communicates a tacit disdain for individualistic propensities: 'the Chinese term for *individualism* (geren juyi) is understood to mean something closer to *selfishness*' (Pomerantz, 1991, p. 8). I think it's safe to assume 'geren juyi' is not meant to be a compliment. What is more, in traditional Asian cultures an autobiography (an 'I' book) is still somewhat of an unwelcomed novelty. "In written Chinese, prose or poetry, the word 'I' almost never appears…Even written in English, an 'I' book by a Chinese would seem outrageously immodest to anyone raised in the spirit of Chinese propriety"(Pillemer, p. 199). "…for a scholar to write a book about himself would have been deemed egotistical in the extreme"(Kim, 1990, p. 153).

Our culture, however, cherishes the pioneering spirit. One only has to read two or three typical lists of American heroes to notice the broad make-up of discoverers, founders, inventors, explorers, and geniuses who deviated from their peers to produce the new and profound statesmen, entrepreneurs, and a few martyrs, as well. Such people were those who defined the 'I' because they could not be average. They could not be common. I am reminded of another remark Charleton Heston made during the same speech. "I believe in the uncommon man maybe because I've played so many of them…we have good men, many famous men, but they are not great men. Great men are suspect in this day and age." Great men and women are suspect in this day and age because they are "distinguished"; they stand out in purposeful ways different from shock jocks and outrageous athletes who thrive on shock-value.

The threat to patriotism comes through Openness' emphasis to be less different and 'distinguished' (as many speakers are introduced[xli]) and more alike and collective; to be less self-reliant and more group-oriented; to be less independent and more interdependent; less of *me* and more of *we*. The Japanese have a saying: "a nail sticking out invites hammering down." But as Sammy Davis, Jr. sang, "I've **got** to be me!"

Individualism is the American way. We are not meant to be 'just like' everyone else lest we become as domestic cattle. Quoting Kant, "These placid creatures will not dare take a single step without the harness of the cart by which they are confined."[106] When individuality is threatened our American way of life is threatened. I see the implementation of Openness, in this case through the agency of political correctness, as the latest form of collectivism. For that reason, I fail to see how it does **not** disturb the patriotic value of individualism.

The second component of American patriotism is a free-enterprise state. The individualist develops to his full potential through the opportunities provided by capitalism. Our faculties and wits are an extension of our individuality. Capitalism is the ideal model of economic freedom. Under it, individuals and groups of individuals can market and profit from their skills, ingenuity, and talents. The individualist is not

---

[xli] Have you ever noticed that Americans introduce speakers as being "distinguished"? This is part of the well-known phenomena that Westerners focus on people being different. (Triandis et al., 1990, p. 1018.).

bound to his brother; his financial potential is not, by custom, limited to that of the slowest among him.

There is a strong connection between economics and individualism. According to an investigation done by Harry Triandis and colleagues (1990), affluence is a major antecedent of individualism.

> "As people become affluent, they become financially independent and independent from their ingroups...Complex cultures (such as industrialized societies like the U.S.) tend to be more individualistic than simple cultures because there are many potential ingroups and individuals have an opportunity to choose whether to stay in or leave these ingroups [parentheses added]."[107]

It was reported that a country's rank, based on one researcher's individualism score, positively correlated with gross national product per capita (Hofstede, 1980). Having lots of money and dozens upon dozens of opportunities to gain more of it, clearly is not the only determinant of individualism. Nonetheless, money is a key antecedent of individualism as affluence affords one many freedoms—whatever they may be. The freedom granted under capitalism is threatened by the opposing ideology of collectivism.

Collectivism, an ideal system in which the means of production are collectively owned and democratically allocated by the organized producers themselves, upholds the motto *one for all*. Resource industries such as coal, lumber, oil, and iron, will be owned collectively by the people and government. The government will regulate even those few enterprises that will remain private. Supporters of collectivism contend that taking over a free-enterprise state would insure a "more perfect freedom to evolve, equal economic opportunity for all, minimization of class conflict, better products at less cost, and security from physical want."[108]

Virtually every fashion of collectivism stresses pure equality; everyone labors the same, is paid the same (according to need), lives the same, and succeeds or fails together. *One for all* means either everyone is rich or everyone is poor. But what of this thing we call pure equality? Is it reachable; and if real equality can be realized and grasped then we must ask ourselves if the means to the ends are desirable. Collectivists like socialists, and proponents of Openness will not falter or fail to relate law with charity and indiscriminateness with justice (e.g., American Civil Liberties Union). To them real equality is more than an ideal. It is something that can and must be brought to fruition by any means necessary.

But we live in a democracy, are we not to steadily strive for equality and civil rights? Is not equality the banner, the song, the soul of the state in a democracy? To both questions, yes. First, however law must be blind justice and not a bleeding heart, making "being offensive" a crime. Secondly, any government or country operating such conditions would be nothing less than utopia where liberty means conformity and competition, maladaptiveness; public means harmony while private, the stark opposite.

The precision it would take to enforce this United States of Heaven would not do with our American way of life (especially the often touted first amendment) and would be too much trouble to establish. You cannot plan an economy.[xlii] Look at any land where, say, socialism or communism thrives and you will not see variety. In these lands, change typically comes only through revolts. Utopia is not something to strive for. Utopias are impractical, restrictive, and to be shunned by all lovers of liberty. Some minds like F. A. Hayek, for one, believed societal structures are best when they come by result of spontaneous order.

> "That even an order which rests on made rules may be spontaneous in character is shown by the fact that its particular manifestation will always depend on many circumstances which the designer of these rules did not and could not know."[109]

[xlii] As Friedrich A. Hayek understood. See the first volume of *Law, Legislation, and Liberty* (Chicago, 1973), 49: In none but the most simple kind of organization is it conceivable that all the details of all activities are governed by a single mind.

The natural instinct for freedom that Charleton Heston spoke of is suppressed and retrained. Under the collectivism doctrine, "we" is more beloved than "I." "We" is paramount for there is no recognition of individual rights. No man has the right (or as collectivists would say, "the need") to live better than his brothers.

Collectivism is no new menace to this country. During the 1930s, many citizens had grown disillusioned with America. The unbridled flapping and arrogant overindulgence of the roaring '20s eventually gave way to economic disaster. Suddenly a lot of people fell hard from their high life, high swinging, high windows. The uninhibited bliss of the times caused Mark Twain to dub it the Gilded Age. With only the enormously wealthy elite left partying (e.g., John D. Rockerfeller, William Randolph Hearst, J. P. Morgan) the contrast between the scant have's and the vast have-not's became stark, and fancies of communism reared their ugly heads among the unemployed 'working' class. The masses saw that only a very small number of people were still living the good life. They grew resentful of capitalism. They felt betrayed by democracy. Now, communism sounded so right and the 'workers of the world' began to protest, sabotage, and strike. Our defeat of communism in our land (one of the highly underrated achievements of the century) enabled us to remain a capitalist society. The collectivism of choice today, that is, what I see as the more pronounced menace, is socialism. Is it a coincidence that the social sciences have within the last decade or so increasingly emphasized cultural, multicultural, ethnic, and gender courses in college?

Socialism seeks to make us all the same. It seeks to make us our brother's keeper. Socialism is the antithesis of capitalism and the ideal vehicle of Open-minded. It discourages the drive to excel, to blaze trails, to outdo others. In short, it discourages competition. Whereas the capitalist emphasizes competition, achievement, and pleasure, the socialist harps on obedience, group integrity, and conformity.[110] Socialists believe public ownership of nearly all of the means of production as well as important utility services, banking and the postal system will bring forth true equality. Socialism stresses acting in the public's interest as opposed to self-interest. It is recognized, though, that people do not always aid others of their own volition. It is likely that many people would have to be forced to act in the public's interest. As Sigmund Freud wrote in *Civilization and its Discontents* (1930), "The contentment that arises from work is only genuine if the professional activity is freely chosen."[111] If we agree that liberty means competition then we are in agreement on this: take away force and all collectivism would not work.

The socialists would have us believe it is unnatural to work under the conditions of capitalism. In contrast, I contend that capitalism better reflects human nature than socialism does because acting in one's self interest is a universal human trait.[xliii] Naturally if man wants something, then he will work (of his own will) to obtain it. Furthermore, socialism achieves what it does at the price of individual initiative. It has the undisputed nature of lowering worker morale because it offers no incentives or benefits based on individual performance. Think about it: if everyone, regardless of effort or achievement, is given the same salary, then we would have a society in which hardly any sensible mind would choose to work at all. This point is nicely illustrated in *Atlas Shrugged* with the example of the Twentieth Century Motor Company. As a result of the motor company enforcing a collectivist policy, the employees slowly but surely become uncooperative, lazy, and they purposely damage work equipment because they finally realize the side effects of disowning self-interest. It pays to read the fine print. Reader, taking the same concept and putting it into the context of education, can the same not also be expected in lowering expectations and standards in our classrooms?

Though man is no primitive, beastly animal species, if we are to apply John Mill's concept of a market full of individuals, the "survival of the fittest" theory would have relevance. Since there are not enough jobs for

---

[xliii] This is clearly a Western point of view. Then again, we are talking about a Western country

everyone, each man must, then, use whatever ability he has in order to gain an advantage over the competition and hopefully secure a job. The individuals who exert what it takes—ambition, experience, diligence, reason, skills, et cetera—will presumably get the job and "survive." The rest will have to try harder the next time. In a capitalist society, the existence of equal opportunity provides the incentive of self-interest to compete.

More, socialism not only affects the pocketbook. It also affects the soul. It weakens one's vitality and makes one purposeless. In a 1964 interview with Playboy magazine, Ayn Rand asserted that the man who has no purpose, but has to act, acts to destroy others. She likened such a man to villains like Joseph Stalin, Adolph Hitler, and the fictious James Taggert. While these three men were of station and power, the sentiment is not exclusive to authority figures. The same is true of any individual who has to act without purpose, including the working man; the masses. For a less dramatic perspective on the effect of socialism, Kant defined enlightenment as "man's release from his self-incurred tutelage." In other words, one's mind and spirit is enlightened, freed, and independent when he is capable of and asserts the courage to use his reason without direction from someone else.

Like socialism, Openness does not entertain differentiation. Uniformity—parity—is an absolute. Because of its collectivist policy, the fictious Twentieth Century Motor Company demands self-abnegation and unchallenged uniformity of its workers. The effect this has on the individual's character and mind is adequately stated by Adam Smith who penned in *The Wealth of Nations*, "The man whose whole life is spent in performing a few simple operations of which the effects are perhaps always the same has no occasion to exert his understanding…He becomes as stupid, as it is possible for a human creature to become…incapable of bearing a part in any rational conversation…"[112] In truth, this is not exclusive to collectivism for the banality of one's life can hinder becoming enlightened within any system.

Since socialism affects the soul of the person, restricting the person's vitality as well as his economic potential, what are we to make of government social programs? Senator John Ashcroft of Missouri believes he sees the ills of widespread social programs: "The '60s called for illegitimacy and dependency, and the rate of welfare accommodations sky-rocketed. We must elevate the highest and best; not accommodate the lowest and least. When government decides to be the keeper of the poor, it keeps them from being anything but poor."[xliv] The powerful effects of government welfare programs do appear to be the cause of dependency and unimpressive work ethic. Then again, it is erroneous to seriously contend the majority of welfare recipients do not work simply because they like being on dole. As Reverend Jesse Jackson frequently points out, the bulk of welfare recipients in the inner cities do work and may not be particularly content with living on welfare checks. But the fact still stands that they remain poor.

What appear to be conflicting sentiments from the senator and reverend are, upon closer inspection, nearly identical. On the one hand, we hear the senator saying welfare accommodations cater to the least because they encourage irresponsibility and laziness, citing the 1960s appeal to illegitimacy and dependency. Speaking at the Quixtar 2000 Extravaganza he reiterated, "We cannot be a culture that emphasizes our lowest and least.

We must elevate our culture to its highest and best." On the other hand, Reverend Jackson stresses that many inner-city people are reliable workers who put in long hours and, yet, still meet requirements for government welfare. Therefore, welfare programs do not necessarily condone poor work ethic because many welfare recipients are dependable workers who take responsibility for their families, and labor to provide for them. And, welfare programs do not better or help qualified citizens

---

[xliv] Senator Ashcroft delivered a speech at Quixtar Extravaganza 2000.

because recipients typically remain 'qualified'. How is that possible? Where is the problem?

The problem is not the people. The people may be lower class but they are not lower life. Nor is the problem government intervention. A government ought to serve and protect its citizens, especially the worse-off of the populace. The problem, the villain, the oppressor in all of this is too much government intervention in the places which tends to breed dependency because folk grow less self-reliant, voluntary effort is retarded. This is characteristic of socialism. A never-ending abundance of social welfare squash the spirit, that is, the vitality, will power, imagination, aggression, of the people they support. Why was there a skyrocketed increase in welfare accommodations in the 1960s? Was it a humanitarian effort due to a national crisis, or was the welfare system being misused?

Reverend Jackson does not suggest welfare programs cease and desist— and for sound reason. As is the case for many families, including those with employed parents, welfare checks just supplement the household income; people don't seriously live off of them (and they surely are not 'living it up!' as many middle and upper class taxpayers like to believe). Nor do I understand him to mean more and bigger government dole. That would only perpetuate the problem of dependency. Admittedly, I am ignorant of the senator's voting track, but judging from his speech I did not gather Senator Ashcroft proposes eliminating all federal government programs like student financial aids, Headstart, public school meals, Social Security, and Medicare so that the true Americans (himself?) can 'pull themselves up by their bootstraps' and rise above the lowest and least. Nor should it be seen that he is referring to the people, themselves, as the lowest and the least.

The commonality betwixt the two perspectives is this: **misuse** and **abuse** of the welfare system will keep poor people from being anything better than poor. (In other words, so long as it's not abused social welfare will improve the situation, further poor people along, right?) Not exactly. (Then, snuff all social welfare and just let citizens live and die in poverty?!)

Not exactly. (Explain!) Certainly. In 19ᵗʰ-century America, before the Great Depression, organizations of neighbors did what could be called social welfare, literally providing aid from cradle to grave. They were called Mutual Aid societies.

I first learned of these organizations at a seminar this past summer on classical liberalism.[xlv] Mutual Aid societies were private welfare—yes, such a thing existed—that provided for their own people. David Beito, historian at the University of Alabama and author of *From Mutual Aid to the Welfare State* (2000), says because these fraternal societies were private and reciprocal there was no stigmatization to using them. Folks did not feel they were "charity cases." After all, the aid was mutual. Self-reliance was strongly encouraged and every fraternal society (they tended to be broken down by race and ethnicity) had strict moral standards. By and large, the associations are gone, just memories, having been overwhelming displaced by the government. Bruce Bartlett, senior fellow at the National Center for Policy Analysis in Washington, reviewed, "Still, Mr. Beito reports, fraternal societies have not disappeared. The Benevolent and Protective Order of Elks and the Moose International, for example, both claim more than a million members. And organizations remain a force in the black community, especially in the middle class.[113]

Speaking to the arena of Quxitar entrepreneurs, Dr. P. James Kennedy said, "Socialism is a disaster. It makes everyone poor. None of it works. It is contrary to the basic rules of human nature and the rules of God." Plainly put, capitalism permits entrepreneurship—the application of our faculties for the production of products—whereas socialism rejects the idea of an individual working by himself, for himself.

The third component of American patriotism is a democratic government. Many times people use the terms capitalism and democracy

---

[xlv] Institute for Humane Studies (IHS) out of George Mason University annually sponsors several seminars and functions on ideas, liberty, and issues central to the substance of libertarianism.

synonymously. This is understandable because history shows that capitalism usually works hand in hand with democracy. It provides a free-market system that provides equal opportunity to gain financial stability. Similarly, democracy is all about the freedom of choice and the pursuit of happiness.

Democracy is a great thing. It works to give each person a voice and a sense that one is crucial, that what one has to contribute does matter. "One man. One vote" shows that the individual has a degree of power in deciding how he wants his government to operate, who he wants to constitutionally operate his government, where he wants his taxes used, what he wishes his representative to support or oppose, and when he wants change. This right of freedom, this attitude of 'I am somebody. I can make a difference', is non-existent or revoked in many other countries. Unlike democracy, socialism and dictatorship do not allow much room for unauthorized self-expression—save for the dictator himself.

Collectivism and dictatorships must needs employ conformity and that conformity comes by way of brainwashing and force. Reason plays no part.[xlvi] People are just clay to fashion as meddling reformers and politicians see fit because it is deemed they are incapable of improving themselves. In *The Great Dictator* (1940) Heir Garbitsch, Secretary of Interior and Minister of Propaganda, is second in command of the fascist regime. Consider his speech finale:

> Democracy, liberty, and equality are words to fool the people. No nation can progress with such ideas. They stand in the way of action. Therefore we frankly abolish them. In the future each man will serve the state with absolute obedience. Let him who refuses, beware.

But we know liberty and equality are not illusions, hoaxes, pipe-dreams. Take away force and all collectivism would not work.

[xlvi] As far as Ayn Rand was concerned, only capitalism and democracy could be defended and validated by reason.

How does Openness threaten patriotism, you ask still? It threatens patriotism by tampering with our ideal of democracy. To reiterate, the *Declaration of Independence* proclaims we all are created equal and we, as a nation, like to believe we hold true to that statement and other similar ones that declare our rights to equal treatment in America.

Yet, you and I know this was not and is not always the case. Only the chauvinist fool does not recognize and acknowledge this nation's history of broken promises, hypocrisy, and racism. Why is it that in spite of the documented racial tension[xlvii] and xenophobia are the contents of the *U.S. Constitution* and the *Declaration of Independence* still hallowed? To put an answer in perspective, below is a narrative shared by Ward Connerly at Hillsdale College's Shavano Institute for National Leadership seminar (*Imprimis,* Feb. 2000):

> I once challenged the proposition that 'all men are created equal.' I said, 'This is phony. I was not born with an equal chance like some other students in college.' Dr. Thompson replied, 'Mr. Connerly, it's not the reality of equality that matters; it's the aspiration of equality that really matters. What's important is that you and I believe that we are equal and the nation continues to perfect that idea.

From this excerpt we gather, it is the ideal of democracy—the "dream"—that we continually strive to make a reality[xlviii]. Admittedly, I dislike and

---

xlvii "The problem of the color-line is the problem of the 20th century," said sociologist and NAACP founder, W.E.B. DuBois.

xlviii Friedrich Hayak in *Law, Legislation, and Liberty,* vol. 1: It is not to be denied that to some extent the guiding model of the overall order will always be an uptopia, something to which the existing situation will be only a distant approximation and which many people will regard as wholly impractical. Yet it is only by constantly holding up the guiding conception of an internally consistent model which could be realized by the consistent application of the same principles, that anything like an effective framework for a functioning spontaneous order will be achieved. Adam Smith thought that 'to expect, indeed, that freedom of trade should ever be entirely restored in Great Britain is as absurd as to expect an Oceana or Utopia should ever be established in it.' Yet seventy years later, largely as a result of his work, it was achieved. (Chicago, 1973): 64-65.

disagree with Ward Connerly on most everything yet the above statement is powerfully befitting because it hits the proverbial nail on the head. This brings us back to my initial point that Openness, more accurately its relativism, threatens democracy because efforts in the name of Openness work to eliminate distinctions with the hope of *making* us all the same. In making us all the same, which is very different from providing equal opportunities, judicial due process, and equal representation, there is a shift from individualism to collectivism. It is subtle because it is guised under philanthropic programs. To expound on the potential threat that some, perhaps well intended, efforts of Openness pose to democracy, I enlist two important discussions: Allan Bloom's critique of the misinterpretation of the *Constitution* and Ayn Rand's perspective on unethical bars on man's rights.

We begin with Mr. Bloom and his book, *The Closing of the American Mind* (1987). The success of a nation depends greatly on having citizens who are in accord with the respective political system. For instance, "aristocracies want gentlemen, oligarchies men who respect and pursue money, and democracies lovers of equality." For citizens to be supportive of a democratic "regime" there needs to be an egalitarian education that produces the qualities (i.e., "tastes, knowledge, and character") essential for exemplifying the *Constitution* and knowing the history of a nation that is "dedicated to the proposition that all men are created equal." Bloom believed that appealing to each man's reason was the goal of the education of the democratic man.

Are today's history instructors imparting the same democratic education? Bloom didn't think do: "The recent education of openness has rejected all that...It is open to all kinds of men, all kinds of life-styles, all ideologies. There is no enemy other than the man who is not open to everything." Amidst our current education there is a (in-coincidental) de-emphasis on natural rights and an overemphasis on cultural relativism so much so that U.S.A. ethnocentricity is being understood as essentially flawed and selfish. Citing relativism as the only virtue of Openness, Bloom posited that this sort of absolutism was effectively causing citizens (i.e., students) to be more fearful of intolerance than error. *There is no enemy other than the man who is not open to everything.*

"But when there are no shared goals or vision of the public good," asked Bloom, "is the social contract any longer possible?" Good question: Is the social contract any longer possible when so many of my classmates, relatives, and people I meet at workshops and elsewhere believe truth is relative? Do you, reader, take diversity—ethnic, political, ideological, whatever—to mean that truth is relative and that relativism is the hallmark for a free and open society? Our rights doctrine trumpets the ideal that all men are created equal not the supposition that all men must be liked and respected. It is by no contract that one must appreciate another because the other is different any more than one must appreciate another for being more alike. "The Constitution does not promise respect for blacks, whites, yellows, Catholics, Protestants, or Jews. It guarantees the protection of the rights of individual human beings."[114] To get an idea of the consequence of misapplication of law let us consider some words from Nietzsche. For it is the fate of every myth, he said, to creep by degrees into the narrow limits of some alleged historical reality and to be treated by some later generations as a unique fact with historical claims.[115]

In the big scheme of things, Openness—relativism and absolutism—basically evokes indifference and therefore does not really open people's minds. Consequently, if our minds are not open—free—then are we truly living in a democracy? Are we honestly individualists? "Openness used to be the virtue that permitted us to seek the good by using reason," wrote Bloom. "It now means accepting everything and denying reason's power." To explain further, the absence of reason renders the Constitution null and void, replacing democracy with an undemocratic regime, and individuality with conformity. Consider Bloom's supportive insight:

> Actually openness results in American conformism—out there in the rest of the world is a drab diversity that teaches only that values are relative, whereas here we can create all the life-styles we want.

Our openness means we do not need others. *Thus what is advertised as a great opening is a great closing* [italics added]."[116]

Another school of thought critical of anything—man, government, religion, human emotion—that caps man's potential and individuality is Ayn Rand's philosophy of Objectivism.[xlix] Briefly, the Objectivist ethics hold that man exists for his own sake, that the pursuit of his own happiness is his highest moral purpose, that he must not sacrifice himself to others, nor sacrifice others to himself. Therefore, Rand contended anything that invaded the realm of man's natural rights (e.g., freedom of mind, speech, and press) also hindered individualism along with reason, which she held as man's basic tool of survival. When a ruling body threatens the self-reliance and independence of its citizens, then we have a clear sign of too much government. Let us refer to this government intervention as an unethical bar on man's rights as legislated opportunity.

Legislation, by definition, means to pass laws. Legislating opportunity thrives under socialism, for example, because of its befitting collectivist principle of acting in the public's interest. However, it would not (so quickly and easily) function in the democratic U.S. because our capitalist society does not require individuals sacrifice their rights and freedoms for the sake of the public. Our system is not premised on charity. There is

---

[xlix] *The Objectivist Newsletter* (January 1962):

"Objectivism is a philosophical movement; since politics is a branch of philosophy, Objectivism advocates certain political principles—specifically, those of laissez-faire capitalism—as the consequence and the ultimate practical application of its fundamental philosophical principles. It does not regard politics as a separate or primary goal, that is: as a goal that can be achieved without a wider ideological context.

"Politics is based on three other philosophical disciplines: metaphysics, epistemology and ethics—on a theory of man's nature and of man's relationship to existence. It is only on such a base that one can formulate a consistent political theory and achieve it in practice...Objectivists are *not* 'conservatives.' We are *radicals for capitalism;* we are fighting for that philosophical base which capitalism did not have and without which it was doomed to perish." Taken from *Capitalism: The Unknown Ideal* (1966), vii.

little pressure to suggest you seriously be your brother's keeper. One is not forced to produce, work, and live up to a false and idealistic happiness established by some legislature. Legislating opportunity has two principal dangers: one, it stifles man's ambition, and two, it stifles man's abilities. The latter can not sharpen without the former.

In crippling the ambitious drive of an individual, the system can more easily control the person. This is because the person has forsaken all reason, purpose, and self-esteem. His catalyst of expression is geared in neutral and can be manipulated this way or that. The powers-that-be can deem it unlawful to express an opinion and no one would object to it. No one will advocate any other views save those given to him or her. No one will harbor a purpose to do any other jobs but those given to him or her. No one will live for more than one is told he or she is worth. Individualism is greatly hindered. So, reader, can you reason independent views? Do you harbor a purpose to work a job that brings you satisfaction? Do others determine your self-worth?

In *Atlas Shrugged*, Hank Rearden, an industrial entrepreneur wages a standoff against excessive commerce regulation when he finds his opportunities legislated. Hank Rearden is ambitious; a pure individualist. The powers-that-be fears him for his opposition, determination, volition, and strength. When blackmail and political intimidation fail to destroy Hank Rearden, the Unification Board eventually legislates opportunity which literally paralyzes the ambition to move forward. It is *ambition* because Hank Rearden has a purpose, to not just produce but to produce his way, using his patented methods and formulas; it is his life. If Ms. Rand was correct about production being the application of reason to the problem of survival, then a legislature on opportunity is anti-life. For that reason, legislating opportunities is an attempt to destroy the real life Hank Reardens of the world.

Legislating opportunity also stifles ability. Imagine an individual is in an empty room. The room represents the world as the individual exists in it. Opportunities are like doors. Abilities are the efforts—physical and mental—necessary to open the doors. Without the doors (opportunities), the individual remains trapped in the room (the existing state). His abilities ebb because they have not been stimulated or used. The individual in the empty room cannot conceive of an exit because he has been taught that one does not nor can exist. He cannot conceive of an escape because he physically can not see one. Are you that trapped individual? The power to reason is hindered when opportunity is legislated.

Hank Rearden is one of many important characters in *Atlas Shrugged*, but the protagonist is John Galt. I will use this character to show how ability is endangered by legislated opportunity. John Galt personifies what Rand considered the "ideal man." Scientist, engineer, and philosopher, John Galt has a complete balance of mind and body, enabling him to formulate strategies and, what's more, act on them. Her protagonist possesses all the virtues of egoism. He is a pure intellectual. As such, he bases everything on reason (otherwise he would be acting without purpose). Rand clearly expresses her philosophy through John Galt.[1] To break—yes, break!—John Galt it is imperative to break the tools of cognition, of reason.

In respects to ability, legislating opportunity is an attempt to destroy the real life John Galts of the world. Legislating opportunity is a tactic of the weak-minded and insecure to destroy those rational and capable from production and directing the world. Once it is realized that the ability to reason translates into power and survival, an undemocratic governing council (represented by the Unification Board in the novel) will work to brainwash the intelligence of its citizens. According to Ms. Rand, reason is man's basic tool of survival and rationality is his highest virtue. Like the Unification Board, Openness' misguided efforts are undemocratic—unpatriotic—because the efforts albeit with good, philanthropic intentions unethically bar man's rights. They seem to mitigate the

---

[1] At one point in the novel, John Galt advises another character, "If any part of your uncertainty is between your heart and mind—follow your mind"(746).

achievements and aptitude of the capable few for the esteem of the incapable lot. Ms. Rand suggest fear, envy, ignorance, or a mixture of each prompts such action. Since reason is man's survival, a "moratorium on brains"—i.e., legislated opportunity—translates into a death sentence for men and women of intellect and purpose.

For many, individualism is more of an illusion than a fact of life. Students of Openness 'argue' truth is relative but they cannot defend 'their' argument as a result of never applying reason, and, therefore are not thinking independently but, in truth, conforming. Conformity is the hallmark of collectivism. Collectivism relies on force not reason. To close, legislated opportunity is anti-life and anti-success and, hence, dangerous to democracy.

Having reviewed three components of patriotism—individualism, capitalism, democracy—I will briefly explain the need for government lest the reader be left with the impression that any and all authority is bad, that any and all authority is an enemy to liberty. We as a nation cling to the concept of freedom—but not absolute freedom. This is why we have an active Constitution and laws. Reasonable citizens understand that anarchy would destroy the state. And some of us understand that some things are more a matter of privileges and political demands, not rights. We want the freedom to protest injustices; to express our concerns through art and the vote; to worship as we please, and to protect our person and property. To put it very succinctly, Americans do not expect unlawful prohibitions to their rights of life, liberty, and the pursuit of happiness. On the other hand, absolute freedom is not wanted because it is equivalent to anarchy *id est* the very threat to life, liberty, and the pursuit of individual happiness. No civilized nation, including the world's superpower, can run without law as a social institution. Roscoe Pound believed law exists to maintain and further civilization with the end being justice. To him this meant the law:

if they cannot satisfy all the claims that men make upon them, at least go around as far as possible. This is what we mean when we say that the end of law is justice. We do not mean justice as an individual virtue. We do not mean justice as the ideal relation among me. We mean a regime.[117]

And more specifically:

I am content to think of law as a social institution to satisfy social wants—the claims and demands and expectations involved in the existence of civilized society...[118]

To have no government would not make us any more of a democracy. It would make us less of a democracy and, moreover, less of a civilized society.

The world is not comprised of only good law-abiding people, and so for a nation to stand there absolutely must be law and order. There must be just rules of conduct. Surely we could not permit citizens to just go "postal" whenever they got upset or were offended, or else there would not be many of us left alive. Let us recognize that man has the natural aggression to seize upon and gratify his immediate desires and needs while at the same time he possesses the equally natural inclination for communion and inclusion. Reasonable and unpsychopathic persons know they must at times curb—sacrifice— their wants, i.e., individuality-ness, for the sake of cooperating with social norms, morals, and other people. Mr. F. A. Hayek sees adherence to certain rules of conduct or collaboration with others inherently essential to social order:

The question which is of central importance as much for social theory as for social policy is thus what properties the rules must possess so that the separate actions of the individuals will produce an overall order. Some such rules all individuals of a society will obey because of the similar manner in which their environment represents itself to their minds. Others they will follow spontaneously because they will be part of their common cultural tradition. But since, although it would be in the interest of each to disregard them, the overall order on which the success of their actions depends will arise only if these rules are generally followed.[119]

A very popular argument over the proper function of government or law is that it should punish injustice and protect the rights of lawful self-defense of property and person. A civilization will not flourish without some give-and-take from its citizens, some mutual exhibit of restraint and respect. This is what being "civilized" entails. We cannot be a nation of citizens running solely on instinct. At this point some positivist will chime, who will make the laws?, as if some backroom in Anytown, USA held the meeting site for the Elders of America. While it is true man never existed without laws that he obeyed "he did, of course, exist for hundreds of thousands of years without laws he 'knew' in the sense that he was able to articulate them."[120] A classic argument on the necessity of law and order and the consequences thereof may be read in Sigmund Freud's *Civilization and Its Discontents* and in several writings by Roscoe Pound on sociological jurisprudence and social engineerings. A democracy does not mean each person is his own government with rights and liberties independent of everyone else's. "For the resulting order to be beneficial," argued Mr. Hayek, "people must also observe some **conventional rules** [boldface added], that is, rules which do not simply follow from their desires and their insight into relations of cause and effect, but which are **normative and tell them what they ought to or ought not to do.**"[121] Being cooperative does not make one a Hitler Youth. We do not have to have uniformity to have unity. Unity is the fundamental part of what we need for America to be a great country in the next century and we can have unity without shifting to collectivism[li] or philanthropic 'justice.'

A classic and thorough explanation of Law and the proper function of government can be found in *The Law* by Frederic Bastiat. Time spent in reading this particular work by Bastiat would be well invested.

[li] Most befitting at this juncture is one of the speeches from John Galt:

"*Rights* are a moral concept—and morality is a matter of choice. Men are free not to choose man's survival as the standard of their alternative is a cannibal society, which exists for a while by devouring its best and collapses like a cancerous body, when the healthy have been eaten by the diseased, when the rational have been consumed by the irrational...Just as man can't exist without his body, so no rights can exist without the right to translate one's rights into reality—to think, to work and to keep the results— which means: the right to property" (Rand, 986).

[100] *The New Left*, 30.

[101] *Closing*, 26.

[102] Ibid., 34.

[103] D. B. Pillemer. Personality and personal event memories, Autobiographical Memories. In *Momentous events, vivid memories*. 194: 1998c.

[104] Triandis, 509.

[105] Roland, 165.

[106] Immanuel Kant, *What is Enlightenment?*, 1784.

[107] H. Triandis, C. McCusker, and C. Hui, "Multimethod Probes of Individualism and Collectivism" (1990), 1008.

[108] James D. Forman, *Socialism* (New York: Dell Publishing, 1972), 36.

[109] F. A. Hayek, *Law, Legislation, and Liberty; Volume I: Rules and Order* (Chicago: The University of Chicago Press, 1973), 46.

[110] Triandid, McCusker, and Hui, 1990.

[111] Sigmund Freud, author of *Civilization and its Discontents* (New York: W.W. Norton & Company, Inc., 1961), 30.

[112] Adam Smith, *The Wealth of Nations* (1776).

[113] Bruce Bartlett. "Those Are Truly Helped Who Help Themselves," *Wall Street Journal*, 10 July 2000, A30,32.

[114] *Closing*, 33.

[115] *Tragedy*, 75.

[116] *Closing*, p. 34.

[117] Pound, *Social Control*, 65, quoted by McLean, *Law and Civilization*, 218.

[118] Pound, *An Introduction to the Philosophy of Law*, 1922 (printed in 1937 by Yale University Press), quoted by McLean, *Law and Civilization*,219.

[119] *Law, Legislation, and Liberty*, 45.

[120] Ibid, 43.

[121] Ibid, 45.

AFTERTHOUGHT:
TO HUXLEY IS TO FORESEE

My original intent was to end with an essay comparing Openness with Orwellian doctrine; it was to be titled something to the effect of " 'O' is for Orwellian". As the work progressed I came to interpret that, uninterrupted, Openness would likely lead to something more reflective of Aldous Huxley's *A Brave New World* than George Orwell's *1984*. It is not a matter of me having any great insight or psychic foresight; the examples and signs are not hidden. By and large, America's school systems are not producing citizens in accord with fundamental democratic principles. Instead, young minds are filled with catchphrases and foundations of absolutism. The virtuous mission of public schooling to enlighten, to provide knowledge, and to instill patriotism and character in all boys and girls regardless of family income and station is hardly evident. Despite the fact that each child, by law, receives formal schooling, it is no easy task identifying the students who went to school, i.e., participated in class and completed assigned studies, from those students who just went to the school, i.e., meeting friends for lunch and gym class. Of my own peers and classmates, the pronouncement of broken English, slouchy posture, cyclical or flat-out inarticulate reasoning, cynicism, indifference, banal aspirations, and bad hygiene speak volumes of the recent education of Openness. Everything is informal. Everything is a joke.

American youth, in general, are not familiar with repressive parents and school instructors, not really. Our generation is more familiar with being 'offended' and has no difficulty in identifying the offensiveness (the highest of all politically incorrect crimes) in anything. Having been given control of some aspects of our lives since adolescence, we have grown up in relative political bliss and freedom and, therefore, some naïvely invite and call for legislation codes on speech and behavior, on systems that wish to unite us through parity by any means necessary even if that means sacrificing liberty. The liberalism of it all obliges intervention—be it machine, government, or drugs—because intervention makes things easier and is really all they have truly known. It is in this light of being conditioned to the easy and the saline that makes Huxley's unnatural apocalyptic prophecy all too real and forthcoming.

When we succumb to our own mechanized and electronic modern times and embrace legislation, philosophies, and technologies that 'undo' our natural capacities to think, and fellowship then we have reduced ourselves to passivity and egoism.[122] All such gadgets and machines, lifestyles and ideologies, doctrine and legislation that lull convenience—*no need for cognition, no need for the hassles of thinking, no need for human interaction, nor for ever exiting your home and encountering others*—are merely oppressors, albeit attractive ones. Neil Postman wrote, "For in the end, he [Huxley] was trying to tell us that what afflicted the people in *Brave New World* was not that they were laughing instead of thinking, but that they did not know what they were laughing about and why they had stopped thinking."[123] Similarly, with Openness, people do not know what they have an opinion about and why they have stopped thinking.

I hope I have shown how Openness, with relativism and political correctness at the hub, mitigates many dearly held virtues and conventions. The well-intended efforts to establish political correctness in an open society have spawned unintended, ridiculous, and intrusive negative consequences. The (mis)use of the philosophy by the feminist movement and gay-rights activism intrude on traditional ethics and concepts of psychology, biology, religion, and other inappropriate areas like the armed forces. But the nation is not to be for their social experiments. The man of reason is not to give in to "offences," revolving his life around the pervading attitude that his happiness and potential are contingent on those around him.

A vigorous and diverse civil society does not hinder reason. We are not like citizens of Hitler's Reich or Hynkel's Ptomania[124] with machine minds and machine hearts. We are not androgynous beings. We are not robots. We are human beings. Openness' effects justify the Huxleyian fear that the rope of irrelevance will strangle truth. Reader, truth is not relative: race matters, intelligence matters, biology matters, name matters, heritage matters, as does the drive and ability to pursue and achieve.

Finally, America must remain steadfast against cultural relativism that seems to erode students' American ethnocentrism, their sense of patriotism and difference. The ideology, it appears to me, contributes more to divide us than unite us and it fails in its unifying mission for one paramount reason—the enforcement of political correctness forces us to accept their—social reformers—groups and plans directly or indirectly. That is not congruent with a just society. Lovers of democracy will, in time, realize we have been too open for our own good and began reinstitution of Constitutional liberties.

Liberty and Justice must not be afraid to reject legislated philanthropy no matter how well meaning it may be on the grounds that forced association or forced charity is incongruent with a just society. Democracy must not be afraid of totalitarianism. Capitalism must not back-peddle from socialism. The individual Right must not yield to the collective Wrong. Individuality must retain its composure before collectivism. Talent and ambition must resist mediocrity and passivity. Optimism and conviction must challenge cynicism and indifference. Reason must not ally that which is not. As the imposter dictator of

Ptomania implored, "Let us fight for a world of reason...In the name of democracy let us all unite!"

Life is what we make it, always has been, always will be.

—Grandma Moses

THE END

[122] *Amusing Ourselves,* vii.

[123] Ibid, 163.

[124] *The Great Dictator,* prod., written, and dir. Charles Chaplin, 128 mins., Trimark, 1940, film.

BIBLIOGRAPHY

———————▼———————

All About Eve, dir. Joseph L. Mankiewicz, 138 mins., 20th Century Fox, 1950, film.

Anderson, Dale, "If you are a wrestler, read this and give it to your parents," *Wrestling USA Magazine*, Vol. 35, 1 (September 15, 1999): 21.

Barlow, D. & Durand, M, (2nd Ed.), *Abnormal Psychology*, Brooks/Cole Publishing, 1998.

Bartlett, Bruce, "Those Are Truly Helped Who Help Themselves," *The Wall Street Journal*, (10 July 2000): A30,32.

Bastiat, Frederic, *The Law*, translated by Dean Russell, New York: The Foundation for Economic Education Inc., 1998.

Baym, Nina, *The Norton Anthology of American Literature*, (shorter 5th Ed.), New York: W.W.Norton & Company, 1999.

Berger, K. S., & Thompson, R. A, (4th Ed.), *The Developing Person: Through Childhood and Adolescence* (Vol 4, chapter 1), New York, NY: Worth Publishers, 1995.

Bloom, Allan, *The Closing of the American Mind*, New York: Simon and Schuster, 1987.

Bly, Robert, *Iron John: A Book About Men*, Reading, Massachusetts: Addison-Wesley Publishing Company Inc., 1990.

Bruner, James, *Acts of Meaning,* Cambridge Massachusetts: Harvard University Press, 1990.

Clegg, Roger, "Why I'm Sick of the Praise for Diversity on Campuses," *The Chronicle of Higher Education,* (July 14, 2000): B8.

Connerly, Ward, "The Content of our Children's Character," [speech], *Imprimis,* 29, no. 2 (February 2000).

Drukman, Steven, "Danger! Masculinity Crisis!" *Out,* (February 2000): 50.

Du Bois, W.E.B., *Souls of Black Folk,* New York, New York: Penguin Group, 1982.

Dunn, Jancee, "Melissa's Secret," *Rolling Stone,* (February 3, 2000): 40-45.

Forman, James D, *Socialism,* New York: Dell Publishing, 1972.

Freud, Sigmund, *Civilization and Its Discontents,* New York: W. W. Norton & Company Inc., 1961.

Gattaca, dir. Andrew Niccol, 112mins., Columbia Pictures, 1997, film.

Gearhart, Sally Miller, (2nd Ed.) *The Wanderground: Stories of the Hill Women,* Watertown, Massachusetts: Persephone Press, 1980.

Hayek, F. A., *Law, Legislation, and Liberty; Volume I: Rules and Order,* Chicago: The University of Chicago Press, 1973.

Imprimis, "The Content of Our Children's Character," February 2000, Vol. 29, No. 2.

Kant, Immanuel, "What is Enlightenment?" 1784.

Koerner, Brendan I., "Where the Boys Aren't," *U.S. News & World Report,* (February 8, 1999): 46-55.

Marine Corps Times, "Citadel Settles Lawsuit," November 1999.

McLean, Edward B., *Law and Civilization: The Legal Thought of Roscoe Pound,* Lanham, Maryland: University Press of America, 1992.

More, St. Thomas, *Utopia,* ed. Edward Surtz, S. J., New Haven and London: Yale University Press, 1964.

More, Sir Thomas, *Utopia: and History of King Richard III.,* ed. Alexander Young. Boston: Hilliard, Gray, and Co., 1834.

Muscular Development, (September 2000): 56.

Nietzsche, Friedrich, *The Birth of Tragedy and The Case of Wagner,* translated Walter Kaufman. New Your: Vintage Books, 1967.

Packard, Vance, *The Sexual Wilderness,* New York: Pocket Books, 1970.

Patai, Daphne, *Heterophobia: Sexual Harassment and the Future of Feminis,* Lanham: Rowman & Littlefield Publishers, Inc., 1998.

Pillemer, D. B., "Personality and personal event memories, Autobiographical Memories," In *Momentous events, vivid memories,* 194: 1998c.

Plato, *Statesman,* translated by J. B. Skemp, New York: Liberal Arts Press, 1957.

Playboy, "A Candid Interview with the Fountainhead of Objectivism," (March 1964).

Poniewozik, James, "We like to watch," *Time,* June 26, 2000, p. 56-62.

Postman, Neil, *Amusing Ourselves to Death: Public Discourse in the Age of Show Business,* New York: Penguin Books, 1986.

Rand, Ayn, *Anthem,* New York: Signet Book, 1946.

Rand, Ayn, *Atlas Shrugged,* New York: Signet Book, 1957.

Rand, Ayn, *Capitalism: The Unknown Ideal,* New York: Signet Books, 1966.

Rand, Ayn, *The New Left: The Anti-Industrial Revolution,* New York: Signet Non-Fiction, 1970.

Rarey, Matthew, "Manhood in America," *The Wabash Commentary,* (February/March 1999): 11-15.

Rogers, R. W., and Prentice-Dunn, S. "Deindividuation and anger-mediated interracial aggression: unmasking regressive racism. *Journal of Personality and Social Psychology,* 1981, **41**, 63-67, reprinted by Elliot Aronson, (7th Ed.), *Readings About The Social Animal,* W. H. Freeman and Company, 1995.

Smith, Adam, "The Wealth of Nations," 1776.

Sommers, Christina Hoff, *The War Against Boys,* New York: Simon & Schuster, 2000.

Sopko, Mark, "A Homosexual Revolution," *Gary Post-Tribune,* (May 25 2000): D1.

Tavris, Carol, "Why Feminism?" [lecture visit to campus], April 4, 2000.

The Great Dictator, prod., written, and dir. Charles Chaplin, 128 min., Trimark, 1940, film.

The Women's Quartley, (Autumn 2000).

Triandis, Harry C., McCusker, Christopher, and Hui, C. Harry. (1990). "Multimethod Probes of Individualism and Collectivism." *Journal of Personality and Social Psychology,* Vol. 59, No. 5, 1006-1020.

Williams, Lena, "N.C.A.A. Reports Movement Toward Equality of the Sexes," *New York Times,* (November 1999).

Whitman, David, "The Masculine Mystique: Wabash College, one of a dying breed," *U.S. News & World Report,* (February 8, 2000): 55.

Wollstonecraft, Mary, *A Vindication of the Rights of Woman,* ed. Charles W. Hagelman, Jr., New York: W. W. Norton & Company Inc., 1967.

Wrestling USA Magazine. Title IX News. http//www.wrestlingusa.com/titlenine.html., cited 18 March 2000.

Zimbalist, Andrew, "Backlash against Title IX: an end run around female athletes," *The Chronicle of Higher Education* (3 March 2000): B9-10.

ABOUT THE AUTHOR

▼

The author lives in his home state of Indiana. He is a senior at Wabash College.

www.ingramcontent.com/pod-product-compliance
Lightning Source LLC
Chambersburg PA
CBHW061306280526
45784CB00002B/917